P9-BIG-509

ANTON WEBERN

by the same author

ANTONIO VIVALDI

ANTON WEBERN

An Introduction to His Works

by

WALTER KOLNEDER

translated by

HUMPHREY SEARLE

Review in PNM, Spring /Summer 1969.

ML
410
W33K63

FABER AND FABER

24 Russell Square

London

First published in England in mcmlxviii
by Faber and Faber Limited
24 Russell Square London WC1
Printed in Great Britain by
Butler & Tanner Limited
Frome and London

All rights reserved

Originally published mcmlxi
by P. J. Tonger Musikverlag, Rodenkirchen/Rhein
as *Anton Webern: Einführung in Werk und Stil*

© English translation
by Faber and Faber 1968

CONTENTS

7

CONTENTS

TRANSLATOR'S PREFACE

Anton Webern is widely regarded today as the 'father of modern music', particularly by the younger generation, and though numerous articles and symposia have been written about him it is surprising that Kolneder's book is the first full-length study of his music by a single author. Walter Kolneder, born in Wels in 1910, studied composition with J. N. David, conducting with Bernhard Paumgartner, and musicology at the Universities of Innsbruck and Vienna. He was formerly director of the Darmstadt Academy of Music and is at present Director of the Badische Hochschule für Musik, Karlsruhe. His book is partly based on university lectures and radio talks, and contains, apart from a complete chronological survey of Webern's music, a short biographical chapter, an account of Webern's work as an arranger, a study of his personality and a description of the effect of his music on the younger generation after his death. Dr Kolneder is able to destroy a good deal of the Webern 'legend' which has mistakenly grown up in recent years round the composer's name by quoting from Webern's own letters and lectures and from writings of others who knew Webern personally during his lifetime. From my own experience as a pupil of Webern I certainly feel that Dr Kolneder has a true understanding of Webern both as a man and artist and is able to show his real musical qualities as opposed to those of the synthetic figure which the 'legend' has created—one is almost inclined to agree with Stravinsky's remark, quoted on p. 188: 'I would very much like to know if Webern himself knew who Webern was!'

In the translation I have used 'note-series' rather than 'tone-row' for *Tonreihe*, as the former enables one to speak of 'serial technique' for *Reihentechnik*. The page references in the text are to the original publications of the works in question, with the exception of the following books, which have been translated into English: in these cases the page references are to the English editions.

René Leibowitz, *Schoenberg and his School*, New York, 1949.

Hans Redlich, *Alban Berg*, London, 1957.

Die Reihe, Universal edition and Theodore Presser Co.

Josef Rufer, *Composition with Twelve Notes*, London, 1954.

Josef Rufer, *The Works of Arnold Schoenberg*, London, 1962.

Arnold Schoenberg, *Letters*, selected and edited by Erwin Stein, London, 1964.

H. H. Stuckenschmidt, *Arnold Schoenberg*, London, 1960.

Anton Webern. *The Path to the New Music*, Universal Edition and Theodore Presser Co., 1963. Referred to in the text as 'Lectures'.

Thanks are due to Universal Edition for permission to reproduce the musical examples.

H. S.

AUTHOR'S PREFACE

The composer Anton von Webern, or Anton Webern as he called himself after the 1918 revolution in Austria, is one of the most disputed figures in the music of our century, in spite of his discovery by the youngest generation of composers, or perhaps even because of their strong support of his music. The distance between admiration of and complete aversion to his music is extraordinarily great. Stravinsky has summed up the whole tragedy of his life and much of the essentials of his work in the splendid, often-quoted sentences which are all the more important, coming as they do from the most successful composer of the present day: 'We must hail not only this great composer but a real hero. Doomed to a total failure in a deaf world of ignorance and indifference, he inexorably kept on cutting out his diamonds, his dazzling diamonds, the mines of which he had such a perfect knowledge.'[1]

The opposite pole of the appreciation of Webern is shown in a typical passage from a criticism by Otto Müller-Minervo of a performance in the Austrian Cultural Institute in Rome. He called Webern's Concerto Op. 24 'an almost incredible extreme of noise. It was grotesque to see the deadly seriousness with which the musicians and their conductor dedicated themselves to their nerve-shattering task. . . . The doggedness of the musicians stood in an unbridgeable contrast to the *Till Eulenspiegelry* of the concerto, which can only be understood if it is received by its listeners with unbridled humour. Only people who enter into the obviously caricature-like character of such pieces can understand and appreciate them. The vigorous applause by the public showed that it had fully grown up to the situation.'[2]

Between these two extremes one often comes across a certain helplessness in regard to Webern, which finds its expression in not taking any notice of him, in conscious silence or misplaced descriptive phrases. In a retrospective article in *Melos*, the leading avant-garde musical journal, Heinrich Strobel admits 'But Webern

[1] *Reihe*, 2/vii.   [2] *Schweizerische Musikzeitung*, 1958/443.

II

—not even a marginal figure!'[1] And in Hermann Erpf's book *The Nature of Modern Music* (*Vom Wesen der Neuen Musik*), which appeared in 1949, Webern is not mentioned: neither is he in David Boyden's *An Introduction to Music* (1956). In other publications he is dismissed in a few lines. Here and there we find expressions like 'music finally on the verge of dumbness', 'creative silence', 'spiritual anonymity': the composer is called a 'melancholy virtuoso of silence': there is talk of 'flashlight photos of the subconscious'. In ingenious formulae of this kind one usually has the feeling that the authors really do not know what to say and are concealing this in an elegant way.

As early as 1927 Hans Mersmann made a violent critical attack on Webern, though he knew at most half of his works: 'Webern's music shows the frontiers and irrevocable final limits of a development which tried to outgrow Schoenberg's work.'[2] After Webern's death serious doubts about his legitimate heritage were expressed, chiefly by his Viennese pupils and friends. In another connection there was even talk of the 'strait-jacket of Webern' and Hermann Erpf said: 'Anton Webern took the line started by Schoenberg further and pursued it to its logical end. What comes afterwards in this direction is simply imitation.'[3] Against this there are remarks by the younger generation of composers such as Jacques Wildberger's 'Tell me your attitude to Webern and I will tell you who you are.'[4]

If one wishes to form a judgment of one's own among this battle of opinions, one has to study Webern's works intensively; there is no other way. Until recently this presented some difficulties, as Webern's complete works have only been available in print for a few years, and performances in official concerts and those commercially organized to suit the taste of audiences are still very rare. The latter deficiency has now been helped by a recording of the complete works made by the American conductor Robert Craft: in spite of many technical imperfections it is a remarkable achievement, in which film musicians from Hollywood co-operated for two years.

[1] 1958/2.   [2] *Moderne Musik*, p. 20.   [3] *Wie soll es weitergehen*, p. 67.
[4] Donaueschingen programme-book, 1959.

This Introduction is intended to help a study of Webern's work in which aural experience ought not to be a poor second after visual analysis of the score. It is founded on lectures on Webern given at the University of the Saarland in the summer terms of 1958–9, on several talks about the composer and some critical essays by the author.[1] In stressing the importance of the early works special emphasis is laid on Webern's stylistic origins and the way he is rooted in tradition. This is not meant to oppose the younger generation's view of Webern, which is mainly based on his later works, but is intended as a supplementation and 'necessary correction' of a somewhat one-sided point of view—which, after all, is the right of creative youth. In this the author feels himself in agreement with the composer's 'This is music which is in fact based just as much on the laws reached by musical development after the Netherlanders. It does not reject the development which then followed, but on the contrary tries to continue it into the future,'[2] and above all with his teacher Schoenberg: 'I am not so much interested in being a musical terrorist as a natural continuer of rightly understood, good, old tradition!'[3]

[1] See Bibliography. [2] To Willi Reich, 3 May 1941.
[3] To Werner Reinhart, 9 July 1923.

BIOGRAPHICAL SKETCH[1]

As regards the date: don't tie yourself to the exact day! Don't make it an actual birthday celebration, no, no: a performance! Don't even mention it . . . how unimportant, how irrelevant, for God's sake! Grant me this wish without question![2]

Webern was born in Vienna on 2 December 1883, the son of a mining engineer, Dr Karl von Webern. His father's duties in the civil service caused the family to move to Graz, and in 1893 to Klagenfurt. Here Webern went to the 'Gymnasium' and took private tuition for the piano, cello and musical theory. It was typical of the musical atmosphere of his parents' house that his success in passing his final examination was rewarded by a trip to the Bayreuth Festival in 1902. As a result of this important artistic experience he made his first large-scale attempt at composition in the following year, a ballad, '*Young Siegfried*', for soprano and orchestra, on a text of Uhland. In the autumn of 1902 he was accepted at Vienna University to study musicology with Guido Adler and harmony and counterpoint with Graedener and Navratil. In 1906 he completed his university studies as a D.Phil. with a thesis on the *Choralis Constantinus* of Heinrich Isaac, the second book of which later appeared in volume XVI of the *Denkmäler der Tonkunst in Österreich*, edited by Webern. While still a university student he had that vital meeting with Schoenberg which led to his becoming Schoenberg's pupil in the autumn of 1904, together with Alban Berg, who was two years younger. According to Wildgans, his regular lessons with Schoenberg lasted till 1908; Leibowitz and later authors cite 1910. The teacher–pupil relationship soon developed into a deep, lifelong friendship which was as important for Schoenberg as for Webern. Looking back on this time Webern himself said: 'It is now twenty years since I became a pupil of Schoenberg. But however hard I try I can't

[1] See Friedrich Wildgans' Biographical Table, *Reihe*, 2/1.
[2] To Willi Reich, 23 October 1943.

15

perceive the difference between then and now. Friend and pupil: one was always the same as the other.'[1]

In 1908 Webern began his professional career. His first engagement as second conductor of the Spa orchestra and summer theatre in Bad Ischl, where Mahler's career had also begun, was certainly not very inspiring, but showed Webern's competence in routine work. For twelve years, with short interruptions for a stay in Berlin in 1911 and for military service in 1915–16, Webern worked as a répétiteur and conductor in Vienna, Teplitz, Danzig, Stettin and Prague; but in 1920 he finally gave up his theatre career to settle in Mödling near Vienna as a conductor of large male choirs and as a teacher. A position as conductor of the Vienna *Konzertverein*, where he had to conduct popular Sunday afternoon concerts with the minimum of rehearsal time, did not last long. In 1922 he came into contact with the Vienna Education Centre of the Social Democratic Party and began an intensive collaboration with them, with a strong accent on popular education—very typical of Webern's artistic personality. Next, he took over the direction of the Vienna Workers' Symphony Concerts, conducted the *Typographia* choral society, founded a Vienna Workers' Chorus and gave private lessons. Apart from a post which he held for some years as teacher of musical theory at the Jewish Cultural Institute for the Blind, Webern never held a teaching appointment. Schoenberg, then director of a composition class at the Prussian Academy of Arts, wrote in annoyance to Alban Berg on 8 August 1931: 'Really one can scarcely begin to understand that neither you nor Webern have been approached regarding a professorship at the Akademie. But believe me: you need not be sorry; it is they who will be more sorry one day!' In the depressing economic conditions of post-war Austria, Webern could scarcely eke out a living in spite of such varied activities: Schoenberg even suggested him as an 'emergency case from Austria' for an American charitable foundation to support,[2] and two years later Webern thought of leaving Vienna to become Municipal musical director in

[1] *Musikblätter des Anbruch*, August/September 1924.
[2] Letter of 24 April, 1923; see also three letters of Schoenberg's dated 9 July, 1923.

Bochum. 'I really must get out of my present financial insecurity once and for all' he writes on 15 April 1925, to Emil Hertzka, the founder and director of Universal Edition. This publishing firm, which had taken on Webern as a composer and collaborator since 1920, was always ready to help, but it is shocking to read letters like these: 'I entreat you to extend till October the monthly advance of 100 Schillings which you granted me from May to September inclusive! I don't know how I shall survive. Since there has been no change in the way of lessons or other regular employment, all I would have for October is my job at the Blind Institute (200 Sch.) and my fee as chorus master (80 Sch.): i.e., 280 Sch.! In November I have my first concert, a Workers' Symphony Concert—I am performing Mahler's *Klagende Lied* in it among other things: then things will become easier. But October! I ask you again to let me be sent 100 Sch. once more. I am now working on a string trio, which I hope to have finished in the course of the winter. . . . If I could only get into a more independent position, so that I could dedicate myself to my work! . . . What work I could do! . . .'[1]

Later his position improved slightly: in 1927, Webern was appointed conductor and then adviser on modern music for the radio, and he conducted abroad more and more as well, but in 1932 he still complains: 'Perhaps salvation will come for me from these frightful conditions in Vienna.'[2] But when as a result of the political events of February 1934 the Social Democratic Party was dissolved, those cultural organizations which had formed the basis of Webern's public activities were also destroyed. The sufferings of so sensitive a composer from these experiences are shown in a letter of 14 February 1934 to Hildegard Jone: 'The disturbances of the last few days are dreadful and getting worse. It is hardly possible to think. . . . And now again . . . gunfire, machine-gun clatter.' Webern's first inner emigration began: 'However I am working again. . . . The worse it gets, the more responsible our task.'[3] Already a year earlier the political upheaval in Germany had deeply affected Webern: 'What is going on in Germany now

[1] To Emil Hertzka, 26 September 1926.   [2] To Josef Humplik, 4 June 1932.
[3] To Hildegard Jone, 20 February 1934.

amounts to the destruction of spiritual life! . . . Look at our own sphere! . . . Today everything that's going on around Schoenberg, Berg and myself is called "cultural Bolshevism". . . . But that makes it all the more urgent to save what can be saved. . . . The time is not far off when one will be locked up for writing such things. At the very least one is thrown to the wolves, made an economic sacrifice.'[1]

This 'economic sacrifice' foreseen by the composer became a fact after the Anschluss of 1938. Webern lost his position at the radio: 'this job has been liquidated'[2] and was driven more and more into the isolation of a private music teacher completely cut off from the world, whose existence depends entirely on his pupils. 'It's the devil of a situation. At present I haven't a single pupil.'[3] 'Now I have pupils again too: a Dutchman and a Balt have come.'[4] 'But I have to limit my activities because of my lessons, which have now started again: I am only free Thursday and Friday afternoons.'[5] An economic catastrophe was averted by Universal Edition, who employed Webern as a proof reader[6] and commissioned him to make piano scores: 'Just think, now I have to work for U.E., to make a huge fat piano score. So I had to postpone work on the *Cantata* [Op. 29] for a bit, otherwise perhaps it would be finished by now.'[7]

'It is disagreeable to have to say that for the last two weeks I have been tied to the hack work I told you about at our last meeting and it will be the same for some weeks, so that I will hardly be able to get back to my own work before the New Year. . . . It's a very annoying situation. But I couldn't avoid it.'[8] 'I'm afraid I now have to interrupt my work for some time: bread-and-butter jobs compel me to.'[9] Webern was so poor that at a Viennese festival of contemporary music, in which naturally

[1] *Lectures*, p. 19.   [2] To Willi Reich, 20 October 1939.
[3] To Willi Reich, 20 October 1939.
[4] To Humplik and Jone, 7 December 1941.
[5] To Humplik and Jone, 11 October 1943.
[6] 'The U.E. Reader', *Die Reihe*, 2/29.
[7] To Willi Reich, 20 October 1939.
[8] To Humplik and Jone, 7 December 1941.
[9] To Joseph Humplik, 4 September 1942.

he was not performed, he could not afford to buy a ticket and could only listen to Orff's *Carmina Burana* standing at the doors.

In the last few weeks of the war Webern, who had been called up in the air defence corps and sometimes had to live in barracks, fled from the advancing Russians and lived in Mittersill, not far from Salzburg, where, while working on a *Concerto in three movements* which was left unfinished, he heard of the death of his son at the front and the loss of his house in a bombing attack. The end of the war seemed to bring with it a final turning-point in Webern's musical life: he was earmarked for important positions in the reconstruction of Austrian cultural life and received letters from Vienna about far-reaching plans, when on the evening of 15 September 1945 that tragedy was played out in which his life was ended by a shot and all hopes thereby destroyed. A search was being carried out in the house of his son-in-law: Webern went outside the house to smoke a cigarette not knowing that the house was surrounded, and was killed by an American soldier of the occupation full of wartime hysteria, obeying orders too rashly. This event, for long camouflaged as an 'accident' because of the censorship at that time, has been described by Friedrich Herzfeld.[1] That was the end of the life of a composer which in its lack of external success was similar to that of Mozart, Schubert and Hugo Wolf, and which, like the life of Bartók and many others, was wrecked by the dark forces of world power politics.

[1] *Neue Zeitschrift für Musik*, 1958/47: see also Hans Moldenhauer, *The Death of Anton Webern*.

WORKS

THE EARLY TONAL WORKS

Only he who inherits great things can create great things. (Goethe.)

In the years round about 1900, when Webern was undergoing his first intensive musical studies as a schoolboy in the small Austrian provincial capital of Klagenfurt, there was still no organized musical education for young people and no possibilities of getting to know music through the radio or records. However, he had the good fortune to find in his teacher, Dr Erwin Komauer, a progressive instructor, whose tuition in elementary theory and composition also included analysis of contemporary works. These were played at the piano and discussed by teacher and pupil together, and it was certainly not without importance for Webern's development that among these works was Mahler's second symphony which had been performed for the first time in Munich in 1900: however for a long time Webern felt an inner resistance to his work. He wrote to his childhood friend Ernst Diez on 20 February 1902: 'At last had the chance of getting to know a Mahler symphony. I liked it very much. The first movement especially impressed me. Certainly if one plays Richard Strauss before or after it one notices a great difference. Strauss's themes are more splendid, more inspired, more powerful. Mahler's music makes an entirely childish impression, in spite of the enormous orchestral display. For instance he uses two orchestras, no less than ten horns, and quintuple or sextuple woodwind.'[1]

When Webern entered Vienna University after his experience of Wagner at Bayreuth in 1902, he again had the good luck to find a teacher who did not exclude the present from his field of research and teaching. Guido Adler, Professor of Musicology, was in contact with Wagner and Liszt in his formative years and embodied the type of musicologist who from his researches into

[1] *Österreichische Musikzeitung*, 1960/303.

historical periods far apart in time was able to draw conclusions which cut across time-barriers. Besides the actual musicology students highly educated practising musicians attended his Institute, and the latest works, performed by first-class executants, were discussed there. If Webern buried himself in work on his thesis on the polyphony of the Netherlands school, he was not shutting himself up in a distant historical sphere but was studying the continuing relationship between the works of a great period of European music and the experiences of present-day music. From Adler Webern derived a profound historical view of the development of musical language, and Webern's later pupils have always emphasized how in his teaching he derived all the traditional rules of composition and also all modern sound phenomena and even the most personal experiences of composition from their historical background.[1]

Even in his lessons with Schoenberg the chief subject was not the latest works of his teacher but intensive analyses of Beethoven and Brahms. When, after his unfinished Wagnerian ballad and early songs, Webern again entered a period of stronger creative activity about 1906, his first works were entirely classical-romantic in form, while in sound and expression they gradually reached forward into paths which take their starting-point from the works of Reger, Mahler and Strauss which were being written at about this time. Webern spoke about this gradual progress towards a greatly loosened tonality in two series of lectures:[2] 'All the works which Schoenberg and also Berg and I wrote before 1908 belong to this stage of tonality.' And the fermenting, even catastrophic character of these years of search in which new works of his teacher released their fullest momentum, is explained in the second series of lectures:

With all these things we are approaching the catastrophe: 1906, Schoenberg's *Chamber Symphony* (chords based on fourths!); 1908, music by Schoenberg which is no longer in any key. In

[1] See, among others, Fr. Deutsch Dorian, '*Webern als Lehrer*', *Melos*, 1960/101.
[2] *The Path to New Music* and *The Path to Composition with Twelve Notes*, 1932/3, p. 44.

1906 Schoenberg came back from a stay in the country with the *Chamber Symphony*. The impact was colossal. By that time I had been his pupil for three years and at once had the urge: 'You must do something like that too!' Under the influence of this work I wrote a sonata movement the very next day. In this movement I reached the furthest limits of tonality.

Schoenberg was enormously productive at that time. Every time we pupils went to him there was something new. As a teacher, he found it very difficult: the purely theoretical side had given out. With his uncanny feeling for form, in a purely intuitive way, he had tracked down what was not right, struggling enormously.

We both felt that with my sonata movement I had broken through to some substance for which the situation was not yet ripe. I finished the movement—it was still related to a key, but in a very strange way. Then I was supposed to write a variation movement, but thought of a theme for the variations which was actually not in a key at all. Schoenberg called in the help of Zemlinsky,[1] who dealt with the matter negatively.

Now you have an idea of the struggle which surrounded this business. It could not be stopped. After that I did write a quartet which was in C major—but only in passing. The key, the chosen key-note, is invisible so to speak, 'suspended tonality!'[2]

The work mistakenly described by Webern as a quartet must be the quintet for string quartet and piano in one movement, written in 1906, which is included in the recording of the complete works, though it bears no opus number. In its melodic lines as in its piano writing it is derived from Brahms; it is no weak imitation, however, but the best Brahms, apart from the somewhat 'external' stretta ending, which seems as if it were tacked on. The admirable handling of the strings by Webern, a cellist himself, is striking, especially in their contrast with the piano, and in the search for unusual tone-colours, as when string tremolos *sul ponticello* pre-

[1] Zemlinsky (1872–1942) composer, and Schoenberg's only teacher.
[2] Op. cit., p. 48.

pare and establish the piano themes with ghostly accents. Development beyond Brahms is especially noticeable in the harmonic style and in the chromatic penetration of the basic diatonic material. Thus the main theme of this well-constructed sonata movement (though with a much altered recapitulation) begins with a chromatic theme of ten different notes.

Ex. 1

The work was performed in 1907 in a concert of works by Schoenberg's pupils, and evoked this characteristic review from a critic, Gustav Grube:

> Students' concerts are not normally reviewed here. In this case there is something so unusual that I feel I must say something about it. Arnold Schoenberg's school of composition can rightly be called the 'high school of dissonance', since hair-raising things are achieved by both master and pupils in this field. As far as I can judge from short pieces, of the eight pupils there were two whom I felt to have talent. These were Alban Berg and Dr A. von Webern. As with all the pupils, the ruinous influence of Schoenberg's compositions made itself felt with these two. The main theme of the Piano Quintet, not badly conceived, in one movement by Dr von Webern soon became lost in arid confusion. Here and there the players seemed to find themselves together as if by chance, so that one sighed with relief and said to oneself 'at last'. Unfortunately such glimpses of light were few and far between in this chaos. What has been said here about Dr von Webern, as far as the style of composition is concerned, applies to all the others.[1]

According to the dates we have, the dividing line between the production of those works which Webern regarded as his first real

---

[1] *Neue Zeitschrift für Musik*, 1907/963.

opera, and his youthful attempts at composition and student works is not very clear. The opus numbers correspond exactly to the relevant stage of his development:

Op. 1: *Passacaglia for orchestra*, 1908.[1]

Op. 2: *Entflieht auf leichten Kähnen*, 1908.

Op. 3: *Five Songs for voice and piano*, 1907–8.

According to the time of composition at least some of the songs from Op. 3 must have been written before the *Passacaglia*, but were probably considerably altered later. (The opus numbers may correspond to Webern's actual development after all.) In any case, Baruch dates Op. 3 1908–9, Craft 1909, Leibowitz 1909 (elsewhere 1907) and it is possible that Wildgans will revise his date on the strength of the composer's diaries.[2]

Those years are notable for rapid production. Later, Webern became a very slow worker: the remaining twenty-eight opera, in spite of their brevity—or because of it?!—are spread over thirty-seven years. There were also external reasons for this very slow creative process. Webern's often harassed financial position made it necessary for him to expend valuable energy in wearisome and time-consuming teaching. He always kept complaining about this.

Passacaglia, *Op. 1* for Orchestra (1908)

Wouldn't you like to look at scores by Dr Anton Webern and Alban Berg, two real musicians? Webern has a *Passacaglia* in the U.E. which has been successfully performed quite often without arousing opposition and is not quite so 'dangerous'. (Arnold Schoenberg to Josef Stransky, 23 August 1922.)

Webern wrote this orchestral work at the end of his years of study with Schoenberg as a kind of 'graduation piece': its gentle tempo and its length of 269 bars make it the longest single movement in all his works. Its scoring for triple woodwind, 4 horns, 3 trumpets, 3 trombones and tuba, percussion, harp and strings is almost as big as the orchestral apparatus used by Strauss in *Till Eulenspiegel*, but avoids the exaggerated sound effects which were normal at

---

[1] According to Wildgans, *Reihe*, 2/1.

[2] A comparative table of dates of composition for all Webern's works may be found in Karkoschka, p. 49a.

that time, as in Mahler's 'Symphony of a Thousand' (No. 8, written in 1906, first performed in 1910) and Schoenberg's *Gurre-lieder*, written in 1900 and scored by 1911, with an orchestra of 7 flutes, 3 oboes, 2 cor anglais, 7 clarinets, 5 bassoons, 10 horns 8 trumpets, 7 trombones, tuba and 4 harps. In spite of several 'Brahmsian climaxes',[1] which do however show the composer's masterly handling of the expressive medium of a large orchestra, the writing and scoring have something of the clarity and transparency of chamber music. The eight-bar theme is announced by

Ex. 2

unaccompanied strings in pizzicato octaves (Baruch calls it 'veiled exposition of the theme') and is of almost Bach-like structure. With the inspired A flat in bar 4 instead of the diatonic A a wide subdominant region is opened up which is already fully worked out in the harmonic structure of the first repetition and is harmonically productive for the whole form of the work.

Ex. 3

The theme and its harmonization have often been discussed in writings on Webern: Redlich[2] numbers the notes and speaks of an 'eight-note row with one note repeated' which 'is the basis of' the passacaglia; Leibowitz[3] finds a three-part structure in the clear division of the theme into groups of two and four notes, 'the juxtaposition of the three motifs of the theme', and even calls them 'antecedent-consequent, followed by a coda', in which motif 1

---

[1] Robert Craft.   [2] *Berg*, p. 30.   [3] *Schoenberg*, p. 193.

consists of notes 1–3, motif 2 of notes 4–6 and motif 3 of the last
two notes. He puts the B flat an octave lower, thereby robbing
the theme of its characteristic interval tension, discovers that
motif 2 then becomes the retrograde inversion of motif 1 and

Ex. 4

says: 'If all these qualities are due to a great extent to Schoenberg's
very strict tuition, it is no less true that Webern's personality
already manifests itself fully in the choice of intervals for the
theme.'[1]

Here Eimert joins in:[2] 'The first six notes of the *Passacaglia
Op. 1* . . . clearly show that the handling of the thematic material
is proportionally determined: in fact they already contain the seed
of the whole of Webern, who never proceeds by motivic psychological paths but builds a proportioned structure out of reflecting
motif-cells—in these six bars we can hear, like a prelude, the basic
motif of the later monadic architect of mirror-forms, who could
never show the similarity of diverse objects and the diversity of
the similar often and passionately enough.' In his introduction to
the recording of the complete works Craft remarks: 'The passacaglia theme's chromatic structure must also be noticed: 11 of the
12 tones are present in the harmony.' He refers to 'the rests
between the notes of the theme:—silence is an element in the
music of Webern, the perfectly calculated time of "Memory and
desire" inside the music.'

Thus in retrospective analysis, in so far as it can be called
analysis, the twenty-five-year-old Webern of 1908 is falsely presented as a serialist, a refined theme-constructor, a twelve-note
composer and a pointillist or at least an early advocate of these
procedures. It is necessary to make it clear that Webern's Op. 1 is
based on a theme, not a tone-row, which is obviously not the
same thing; that in the whole piece this theme is never divided

---

[1] *Schoenberg*, p. 193. [2] *Reihe*, 2/33.

into three sections and that the motivic relationship dug up by
Leibowitz is probably quite accidental; that in the whole work the
motivic working-out is never produced *from* the theme but is im-
posed *on* the theme or its variant forms as the occasion arises; that
in the music of 1900 and thereabouts, by Strauss and Reger, for
instance, it was not unusual for eleven notes of the chromatic
scale to appear in an eight-bar harmonic sequence of twenty-eight
notes (Gesualdo da Venosa did the same thing centuries earlier
in the narrower limits of only a few chords); and that the rests in
the theme are probably modelled on the finale of the *Eroica*.

Naturally any composer who is granted an organic development in the artistic unfolding of his nature will show some things
in his Op. 1 which only come to fruition later on. Webern was
above all conscious of a real responsibility to the past in facing
the problem of passacaglia form and solving it in a masterly way.
From Schoenberg's strong spiritual roots in the achievement of
Brahms and the important part which the analysis of Brahms's
works played in his teaching, it seems possible that Webern took
the finale of Brahms's fourth symphony as the starting-point for
his conception of an orchestral passacaglia. But he in no way
copied his model, developing this type of form further in a highly
personal way. The theme can clearly be recognized up to the
nineteenth variation, if sometimes considerably transformed:

Ex. 5

In variations 20–23 the theme dissolves more and more and
finally disappears entirely after bar 201. Already from bar 9 (Ex. 3)

and more clearly from bar 17 on one can see the inherent tendency of passacaglia form to let melodic invention derived from the theme dominate over the use of the theme itself.

Ex. 6

Just as in Bach's Chaconne for violin solo, the harmonic scheme divides the whole work into three parts:

Bars   1–96 D minor   97–128 D major   129–269 D minor

Larger sections within these main parts are built up by gradual motivic development and by dynamic means: ppp for the beginning, pp from bar 17, p from bar 30 (in the main part): first major fortissimo bar 56. From the subsidiary parts which appear in bar 9 (Ex. 3) and bar 17 (Ex. 6) two subsidiary themes are gradually crystallized which outstrip the passacaglia theme in importance and form the basis of fairly long episodes, when the passacaglia theme has temporarily or entirely disappeared, from bar 201 on.

Ex. 7

Countertheme I   Variation of above

Ex. 8

and Countertheme II, which appears for the first time in bar 65 in the bass, after gradually developing into a definite shape. This

28

already shows the effect of Schoenberg's idea of a 'developing variation', in which the techniques of Beethoven and Brahms are consolidated into a principle. Ex. 9 shows this development.

Ex. 9

From bar 228, at the climax of the work, the contours of the passacaglia theme are recognizable once again in a seemingly quite un-Webern-like f f f outburst: then the work dies away in a Coda, becoming quieter all the time, which is based on a new version of Countertheme II.

Ex. 10

The 'Meistersinger' counterpoint and concise thematic material, developed out of the very nature of the instruments, which is typical of early Strauss, strongly influenced Webern's melodic writing in this work. In spite of these influences this Op. 1 is a 'masterpiece of the fullest authenticity'.[1]

Entflieht auf leichten Kähnen, Op. 2 1908 for four-part unaccompanied mixed chorus. Text by Stefan George,

Tomorrow, Wednesday, the Hugo Holle choir in Vienna will sing my a cappella chorus 'Entflieht . . .': this chorus has never been done anywhere except this year in Fürstenfeld, a little place in East Styria: so tomorrow is as good as a first performance after twenty years. I wrote the chorus in 1908. . . .' (to Alban Berg, 6 December 1927).

I'll tell you quickly in writing how much your chorus delighted me— in spite of the mediocre performance. What a wonderful melody!! and how beautiful it is when in the reprise the F sharp of the first soprano is first avoided, only to arrive with mysterious power (ppp) at figure 5. Not to mention the low G of the basses. It made me shiver with awe before this mystery of Nature—no, of your art! (Alban Berg to Webern, 8 December 1927.)

The poem, written by George in three four-line verses, was also set by Webern in three parts (A 9 bars, B 9 bars, A 11 bars). Webern the musician's attitude to the text is shown by the fact that owing to the rapid movement of the middle section he actually took the first two lines of the last verse into this section of the work. In order to give the reprise of the A-section—which comes back note for note after a momentary pause—the corresponding proportions, repetitions of the text were necessary: *Es sei die stille Trauer die diesen Frühling fülle es sei die stille Trauer die stille Trauer die stille Trauer die diesen Frühling diesen Frühling fülle diesen Frühling diesen Frühling fülle.*

Webern's early liking for strict construction, clearly modelled on Netherlands examples, is shown in the canonic layout of the composition, of which Stuckenschmidt has said: 'The flight from the "intoxicated worlds of sun" [*berauschten Sonnenwelten*] takes place in the rhythm of a Barcarolle and is portrayed by the use of imitative counterpoint'.[2] In section A the vocal pair of soprano and alto are imitated by that of tenor and bass (in reversed

---

[1] Adorno, *Klangfiguren*, p. 164.   [2] *Schöpfer*, p. 197.

position in bar 1 for reasons of sound). In the middle section the voices in pairs form a four-part canon.

Ex. 11

The work is Webern's last composition with a traditional key signature. A look at the first few bars (Ex. 11) shows that in this style of chromatic alteration each separate chord can still be related to a tonal centre. But the effect in sound at the speed of quaver = 112 is that of a hovering tonality with tonal supports only at the formal divisions. Thus the G major chord at the end has a startling, almost unorganic effect, though prepared for long in advance. How far Webern, in this still tonal work, sometimes pushes hard at the frontiers of total chromaticism is shown by the beginning of the middle section.

Ex. 12

Within the compass of a fifth the lower part contains seven notes of the chromatic scale (C sharp is missing, D is repeated). The answer in the upper part uses the notes which are not used by the lower part, thus almost making up the whole chromatic range: within the sixteen notes of the example eleven different notes of the chromatic scale appear. The setting of the second part of the text ('pale blue dream powers') is built up in exactly the same way. Here there is a clear and conscious use of a principle of composition which later attained a fundamental importance in Webern's works, the principle of complementary harmony. This can affect a series of chords just as much as contrapuntal writing. In a sequence of notes the sounds are harmonically enriched by it and the sequence achieves the greatest tension and strongest 'gradient' as the chords have no notes in common, the sounds complete and complement each other. In polyphonic writing a countersubject is written in such a way as to avoid the tonal sphere of the main subject. Mersmann[1] says about mediant relationships: 'the sequence of C major and E major can no longer be based on a logical principle but is due to the complementary relation of their colour substances'. The strong tension of the opening bars of the *Tristan* prelude rests on this principle.

Ex. 13

The two chords marked are in a complementary relation to each other: together they produce eight different notes. Stucken-schmidt has pointed out the importance of this principle of tension in Reger:[2] he speaks of 'a kind of chromatic osmosis', of 'complementary chordal writing in Berg'[3] and recognizes in the harmonic structure of Schoenberg's Op. 16 and Webern's Op. 10 'chords of many notes, in the progressions and sequences of which the only recognizable principle is that of the avoidance of repetitions of notes'. Complementary harmony is one of the most important means of harmonic and melodic tension in romantic and especially highly chromatic music, it is an essential method for expressionism, and when logically used leads to total chromaticism. Adorno says that 'the law of the vertical dimension in twelve-note music should be called the law of complementary harmony'.[4] In the strong chromatic colouring of a composition which was still tonally conceived Webern's Op. 2 is as important in the development of the composer's style as it is in the history of the development of style in general at the time he wrote it.

[1] *Moderne Musik*, p. 33.   [2] *Neue Musik*, p. 10.   [3] *Schöpfer*, p. 185.
[4] *Philosophie*, p. 53.

THE STEP INTO NEW TERRITORY

The real composer only writes something new and unusual in a new combination of sounds in order to express something new and unusual which moves him. This can be a new sound, but I believe rather that the new sound is an involuntarily discovered symbol which proclaims the new man who expresses himself through it. (Schoenberg, *Harmonielehre*, p. 447.)

With the Five Songs from *Der siebente Ring* (the Seventh Ring) of Stefan George, Op. 3, Webern gave up writing a key signature at the beginning of his pieces: these cannot be related to any tonal centre—only in the fifth song could F be regarded as a fundamental note. With these songs Webern dared to take the step into a new region, the region which is commonly described as atonality. It is well known that this term is meaningless in itself. It has become the most misunderstood catchword in the battle against modern music: Schoenberg rejected it and suggested Pantonality instead, without success. If sound phenomena which are no longer explicable by the tonal systems operating up to that time—particularly the major-minor system—belong to the nature of atonality, this term may be retained and is used here in this sense. Webern himself has spoken of that exciting time of the internal agonies of those years in which each new work meant a stronger disruption of tradition, a step forward into the unknown. It was not at all a question of thinking up new things with the mentality of a small-time art revolutionary, in order to shock the bourgeoisie. Every word spoken by Webern about this period shows rather his fear when faced by new elements bursting in: 'It is not easy to speak about everything we went through then!'[1] 'Naturally it was a fierce struggle, there were inhibitions of the most fearful kind to overcome, a panic fear as to whether it was possible. ... You're listening to someone who has experienced and fought for all these things. All these events tumbled over one another; they came upon us unselfconsciously and intuitively. And never in music has such resistance been shown as there was to these things.'[2]

[1] *Lectures*, p. 54.   [2] *Lectures*, pp. 44

What developed in the music of that time, the later Reger, Scriabin and the youthful works of Bartók, does not stand in isolation. It arose out of the instinctive feelings of the creative generation in the decade before the first world war and has parallels in the visions of colour of the painters known as the *Fauves* and also those of the Dresden *Brücke*, the group of the *Blaue Reiter*, round Macke and Marc. The poets were expressing the hidden ferment of this time earlier than the composers, and it is no accident that the decisive steps were taken by Schoenberg and Webern in vocal works. The biggest stimulus was given by Stefan George, whose poems Schoenberg set when he introduced a soprano voice into the third and fourth movements of his second string quartet in 1907–8. While still working on this quartet he wrote the two songs with piano, Op. 14, also on texts by George, and finally in 1908–9 he set the cycle of fifteen poems from the *Buch der hängenden Gärten* for high voice and piano, Op. 15. In this era, which was of such significance for the development of music, of which Herzfeld said that 'new strata of our being were opening',[1] Webern also wrote his Opp. 2–4 on texts by George. Schoenberg has often said that the decisive impulse came from poetry, for instance in a letter to Richard Dehmel:[2] 'Your poems have had a decisive influence on my musical development. Through them I was compelled for the first time to search for a new sound in lyricism. I mean that I found it without looking for it by reflecting in music what your poems aroused in me. People who know my music can tell you that my first attempts to set your songs contain more of what was to develop in me in the future than many later compositions.'

'With the George songs I have succeeded for the first time in coming nearer to an ideal of expression and form which has been hovering about me for years. Up till then I lacked the power and confidence to realize this ideal. But now that I have finally entered on this path I know that I have broken all the bonds of an outworn aesthetic. . . .'[3]

[1] *Musica nova*, p. 67.   [2] 13 December 1912.
[3] From the programme of the first performance of the George songs, Vienna 1910: Schoenberg's comment.

The works of Webern which were written in the spiritual climate of these years are especially notable for a new kind of sound. Even the first chord of the first song of Op. 3 cannot be understood through the teaching of conventional harmony, and even many more recent attempts at analysis of chords of this kind turn out to be questionable.

Ex. 14

Op. 3, No. I. 1

According to Hindemith[1] the fifth E–B provides the fundamental notes: Wolpert[2] says that notes such as the E flat and B flat are 'split off' from the main notes and calls chords of such notes 'splinter chords'; Redlich[3] also takes as his starting-point traditional chords which are 'darkened' by seconds or 'wrong' octaves. In fact the tonal effect of a structural fifth is also annulled through minor seconds if a note through being placed low makes its overtones permeate the whole. Many people have regarded the abolition—the 'dissolution'—of tonality as the essential point of this new technique of sound, and remarks by Schoenberg and his pupils seemed to support this. But one must be clear that the abolition of tonality is a secondary, a purely technical phenomenon, so

[1] *Craft of Musical Composition.*   [2] *Neue Harmonik*, p. 13.   [3] *Berg*, p. 54.

to speak, the result in sound of interior processes as observed from the outside. Every new sound formation is primarily a question of expression and not of 'compulsion by the pressure of historical development'. Webern himself in an excellent study of Schoenberg's early works, written in 1912, said: 'The experiences of his heart become music. Schoenberg's relation to art is rooted entirely in the need for expression. His emotions are of burning fire: they create completely new values of expression, and so they need new means of expression. Content and form cannot be separated.' And later in the same essay. 'These new sound techniques are born out of the expression of this music.' Minor seconds sounding together are typical of the new world of sound which we meet in Webern's Op. 3. But these minor seconds hardly ever appear in close juxtaposition, thus differing considerably from the 'tone-clusters' of Henry Cowell as well as from the groups of minor seconds which imitate percussion effects on the piano in Bartók and Stravinsky. Webern, who called himself exclusively a lyricist ('I know well that my work still means very little commercially. But this is probably because of its almost exclusively lyrical nature up till now: poems bring in very little money, but they still have to be written.'[1])—Webern always uses these minor seconds in extended positions, whereby he achieves exactly those twilit sounds which seem to him to suit the world of expression of George, and later of Trakl, Rilke and others. To look for remnants of tonality in these sounds is as wrong as to speak of the 'abolition of tonality'. The sound D–F–C sharp–E in bar 3 is not a chord of the ninth on the tonic of D minor with the fifth left out, but a new sound composed of the two units C sharp–D and E–F. The unprejudiced listener hears in the unfolding of the music, not a chord built up of thirds, nor added minor seconds or major sevenths and minor ninths, but sounds in which the individual notes are fused into a unity. The professional musician with his tendency towards visual analysis sticks too much to the individual notes, he sees dissonances and looks for resolutions which no longer follow. Hence the rejection of this music by those who are imprisoned in the traditional methods of studying music.

[1] To Hertzka, 6 December 1927.

The first chord of the song Op. 3 No. 1 is a 'colour sound' of this kind, in which traditional dissonances are fused into a new 'consonance', i.e. a unity of sound. The 'emancipation of the dissonance' of which Schoenberg so often spoke is here fulfilled. This new kind of sound also appears in the part-writing: in the sixth bar the C in the bass stands in the relationship of a minor second to the notes B and C sharp in the upper stave of the piano —at a distance of up to five octaves! This kind of part-writing based on sound appears even more clearly in bar 2: the upper lines of the piano part are in two parts with intervals of a third up to a diminished seventh, the third part has a minor second relationship with the top part, as bass has with the second part. Bars 6 and 7 of the first song show how much this minor second relationship determines the part-writing.

Ex. 15

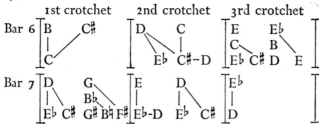

When these minor seconds appear together with other intervals, especially thirds, fourths and fifths, formations of three or four notes appear, but also sounds of four or more notes which are built up of two or more minor seconds: for instance bar 7, 2nd quaver:

$$\overgroup{\text{F sharp–G–G sharp}} + \overgroup{\text{B flat–B natural}}$$

The fundamental importance of these minor second relations in Webern's later works, which is already so clearly shown in his first non-tonal work, suggested a systematic examination of this world of sound; an experimental attempt to find the possibilities of sonorities of several different notes based on minor seconds and to show their effectiveness in creating sounds and building motifs in Webern's works.

THE SCHEME OF WEBERN'S TECHNIQUES OF SOUND

The aesthetic of free atonality is one of the most interesting and least studied problems of modern culture. (H. H. Stuckenschmidt, *Schöpfer*, p. 185.)

As the traditional nomenclature of intervals stems from the diatonic system, from which basic diminished and augmented intervals are derived, it has proved to be too complicated for the study of music which is either based on total chromaticism or is developing towards it. For this reason it is best to count in semitones, starting from the lowest note, which however is not a key-note here.

o	Basic note	6	Augmented fourth, diminished 5th
1	Minor second, augmented basic note	7	Fifth
2	Major second, diminished third	8	Augmented fifth, minor sixth
3	Minor third, augmented second	9	Major sixth
4	Major third, diminished fourth	10	Minor seventh
5	Fourth	11	Major seventh, diminished octave
		12	Octave

Intervals larger than the octave are shown as $12 + 1, 12 + 2$ etc.

In the formation of triads a 'framework interval' is presupposed, though this has no concealed tonal significance. By each note appearing together with the notes a second above and below, four possibilities appear from the minor third onwards of which at least two differ in identity, transposition, inversion or transposed inversion, while from the diminished fifth on all four are different:

Ex. 16

Framework sound   Formation of triads

The different numbers under the same sound give the inversion, e.g.

Ex. 16a

Thus nine triads remain which are different in structure, marked I, IIa, IIb, IIIa, IIIb, IVa, IVb, Va, Vb, of which each can appear in the three forms of the basic position, the first and the second inversion. By the same procedure four-note chords can be obtained in which each 'framework interval' can be joined to two minor seconds simultaneously. As an example here is interval 5, the perfect fourth.

Ex. 17

Sounds of five or six notes can be obtained by joining two-note 'framework sounds' to three or four minor seconds:

Ex. 18

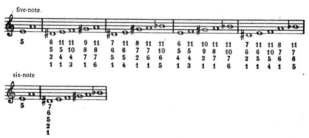

If one starts with three-note 'framework sounds' the possibilities are increased. The sound E–G–C, for example, as well as four-, five-, six-, seven- and eight-note formations produces a nine-note sound D sharp–E–F–F sharp–G–A flat–B–C–C sharp; the four-note sound E–G–B flat–D flat finally enables one to use the full possibilities of a twelve-note chord.

Chords produced in this way can naturally also be extended by other intervals, such as major seconds. The first four bars of the song Op. 3 No. 1 show sounds of this kind.

Ex. 19

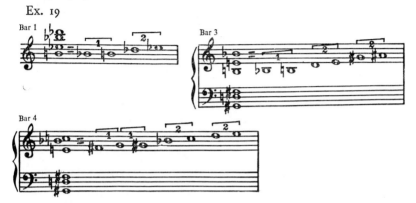

Further examination shows that this method of chord-building is a constant factor in all Webern's works, however much his style may have changed. And it will become clear that his construction of motifs is essentially based on the projection of such chordal sounds in a horizontal dimension. There are various possibilities in the method of writing which can be classified as follows:

a. Chordal sounds
b. Formation of motifs or melodies from the notes contained in chordal sounds
c. Melody and chords together in homophonic writing
d. Polyphonic writing

Once one knows the derivation even of complex chordal formations from basic sounds, important structural components of Webern's writing can be reduced to their elements.

Five Songs from Der Siebente Ring *by Stefan George, Op. 3,* for voice and piano (1907–8)

I   *Dies ist ein Lied für dich allein*
II *Im Windesweben war meine Frage nur Träumerei*
III *An Bachesranft die einzigen Frühen die Hasel blühen*
IV *Im Morgentaun trittst du hervor*
V   *Kahl reckt der Baum im Winterdunst sein frierend Leben*

The music of our time is definitely aiming towards atonality. Yet it does not seem right to regard the tonal principle as the absolute opposite of the atonal principle. In fact the latter is the consequence of a gradual development from the tonal principle, which goes forward step by step and shows no gaps or tremendous leaps of any kind. (Béla Bartók, *Das Problem der neuen Musik*.)

When, after giving up tonality, the 'structural tendencies of harmony'[1] were no longer fruitful for Webern, he clearly seems to have tried to compensate for this by strong motivic relationships in his writing. The first song is an instructive example of how the piano part develops out of the voice part rather than giving a backcloth of sound and atmosphere to a melody which is independent of it. The vocal writing grows entirely out of the declamation of the text: there are no melismata, and with two small exceptions every word of the text corresponds to a note. The high notes in the melody are in the exact places on which the emphasis lies in natural declamation:

'This is a *song* for *you* alone. . .'[2]

Two procedures are recognizable in the construction of the melody: in general there is a recitative-like treatment of the voice, in which mainly small tonal spaces (in the first song, bars 1–4, minor seventh, diminished fifth, perfect fourth) are filled up chromatically, but there are also broad melodic gestures at the climaxes (*Durch Morgengärten klingt es*). It is clear from the following example how seemingly recitative-like phrases are dovetailed motivically in themselves as well as in the relationship between voice and 'accompaniment':

[1] Schoenberg.   [2] Ex. 14.

Ex. 20

The middle section of the song is dominated by a seven-note motif with wide intervals which is imitated by the piano and which provides in various different shapes, the motivic material for the quick-moving lower part.

Ex. 21

Op. 3, No. I. 5

Here the two-note motif, D–E flat appears, an unfolding of the minor second motif in the horizontal over two octaves, which was such a characteristic of late Webern. But note the pedal directions! An analysis of the chordal sounds shows the validity of the types discovered in the systematic examination above.

Webern's mastery of form is shown in his technique of varying the repeat of the A section in A–B–A form by changing round the subsections a and c from the beginning.

Ex. 22

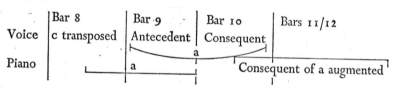

	Bar 8	Bar 9	Bar 10	Bars 11/12
Voice	c transposed	Antecedent	Consequent	
Piano		a	Consequent of a augmented	

This considerable variation embodies a principle which was an essential part of the aesthetics of the Schoenberg school: avoidance of any note-for-note recapitulation. The reaction of the late romantics against classical clarity of form had even led to Mahler's remark that 'Mozart's string quartets were finished for him at the double bar'.[1] In the theory of psychological form construction it is argued that the recapitulation meets the listener in a different state of experience. In his teaching Berg used to say, 'Think what your themes and motifs have lived through in between,'[2] and Schoenberg once stoutly pronounced, 'Don't write a literal re-capitulation, the copyist can do that.' If strictly followed this principle leads to the avoidance of any kind of repetitive effect, and the problems connected with this occupied Webern for a long time.

The first song of this Op. 3 also shows a small detail, but one which is not unimportant for Webern as an interpreter as well as for the interpretation of Webern's music: all three sections of it end in a ritardando, the final one being actually written out. The sections begin again with an exact or modified return to the tempo ('Tempo' and 'a little slower than the beginning'). Incidentally a clear shaping of structural divisions was one of the outstanding characteristics of Webern as a conductor.

The dynamic range of the song, required by the delicately written text, is also striking: p comes only twice in the vocal part as the highest dynamic marking, there are four pps and one ppp, while the piano with nine ppps is kept at an even quieter level. Through pieces of this kind Webern got the reputation of 'the pp composer' early on: 'he is the composer of the pianissimo espressivo'.[3] Webern, shy and reticent as a person, preferred to choose texts in which more is hinted at than said. The fact that he could also 'do other things', and in the period of his greatest preoccupation with expressionist tendencies wrote a song (Op. 17 No. 3) which is almost exclusively f and ff throughout is mentioned here to help correct such catch phrases.

The remaining songs of Op. 3 confirm the points established in connection with the first song. The minor second, mostly in an extended position as 11 or 12 + 1, is the basic interval for the construction of chords almost throughout.

[1] *Österreichische Musikzeitung*, 1960/304.   [2] *Melos*, 1955/40.
[3] Erwin Stein in *The Chesterian*, 1922/35.

Ex. 23

Op. 3, No. III, 13

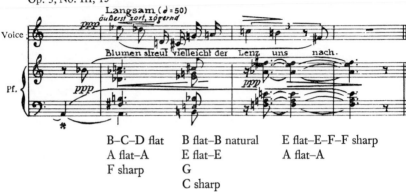

B–C–D flat	B flat–B natural	E flat–E–F–F sharp
A flat–A	E flat–E	A flat–A
F sharp	G	
	C sharp	

A chromatic nine-note melody, three six-note chords in the piano in minor second structure and complementary harmonic sequence (with some repetitions of notes): the minor second group of A–B flat–B natural–C–D flat at the beginning.

If traditional chords are hidden within sounds of this kind, they are concealed by minor seconds and thus not heard.

Ex. 24   Op. 3, No. V, (Beginning)

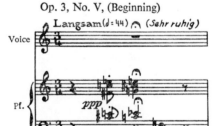

E flat–E–F. Within it F–(A)–C–E flat–G (dominant ninth of B flat with third missing)
C–C sharp
G

Passages with a clear tonal basis, like the fifth bar of the first song with its turn towards the dominant of A minor, are relatively rare.

Melodic construction by small intervals is the rule. But if larger intervals are used at expressive climaxes (in Webern these are

46

usually restrained pp or ppp climaxes) these melodic structures
are almost always horizontal projections of minor second sounds.

Ex. 25   Ex. 26

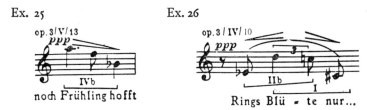

In the conjunction of melody and harmony there are often
tense complementary harmonic formations, for example.

Ex. 27

Voice and piano are dovetailed motivically: in the piano part
there are two seven-note groups, each with three complementary
notes in the vocal part.

The kind of chromaticism shown in the third bar of the fourth
song is astonishing.

Ex. 28

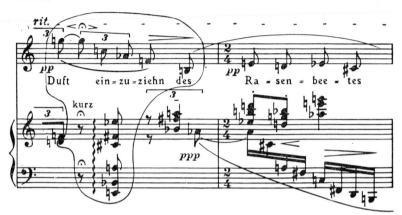

A chromatic sequence of nine notes in the voice part; the six-note
chord in the piano is in a complementary relationship to the first
five notes: the D which is missing from the twelve-note group is
heard just before. The motif at *des Rasenbeetes* is accompanied
in minor seconds in the upper piano part like an organ mixture:
the melodic line with its wide leaps (*Duft einzuziehn*) contains the
minor second relationships G–A flat and C–B and provides the
motivic material for the whole song; for instance in the first bar:

Ex. 29

Op.3, No. IV, 1

See also the lower piano part in Ex. 28, and especially bars 5 and 6
of the song with the pictorial demisemiquaver movement at the
words *Fern fliegt der Staub* (Dust swirls afar).

The second song is constructed in very similar fashion. The
piano figuration (*Windeswehen*—wind blowing) is derived motivically from the broad melodic line of *Nur Lächeln war* and

dominates the first part. A pressing, up-beat motif, of a kind which often appears in Webern's early works, is the foundation for the second half of the song, which ends ff.

Ex. 30

Nun drängt der Mai

Ex. 31

Op. 3, No. II, 9

Five Songs on texts of Stefan George, Op. 4, for voice and piano (1908–9) To Herr Werner Reinhart[1] cordially

I *Eingang*
II *Noch zwingt mich Treue über dir zu wachen*
III *Heil und Dank dir die den Segen brachte*
IV *So ich traurig bin weiss ich nur ein Ding*
V *Ihr tratet zu dem Herde wo alle Glut verstarb*

[1] Werner Reinhart, 1884–1951, was a wholesale merchant in Winterthur who took a big part in the organization of Swiss musical life and was an excellent clarinettist: Stravinsky dedicated his clarinet pieces to him. He was a warm-hearted supporter of contemporary composers, among them Webern. Schoenberg wrote to him on 9 July 1923: 'Webern is in a bad way. He is entirely without an income. Prices are dreadfully high: Austrians cannot help him permanently and we don't know any rich people. I know that you have already done a lot for him. That is why I delayed for so long in telling you this. But as I can't do anything else I think I must do so. Can you do something more for him?' and on 22 August 1923: 'I haven't yet thanked you for the speedy and kind-hearted response to my news about Webern.'

Now as regards the ISCM[1] concert planned for Basle . . . which songs are you thinking of? How important it is to make a good choice! For instance . . . *'So ich traurig bin'* from Op. 4—that has *never* yet been sung!!![2]

Webern himself gave the date of composition of this song cycle in the printed score. Their nearness to Schoenberg's Op. 15, composed at the same time, is unmistakable. Although even in his early works Webern shows a tendency to avoid formal correspondences in small forms, George's eleven-line poem *Eingang* is so laid out in the setting that the clear formal divisions of the motivic content in the piano part provide a solid musical basis for the strongly declamatory voice part:

A   Bars 1–3 with a motif of a second in the piano taken over from the voice part

B   Bars 4–5 with a characteristic motif of a third (*im Blau nur*)

C   Bars 6–9 by a contrasting middle section containing wide intervals (*Korn um Korn auf*)

B1 Bars 9–13

A1 Bars 14–15 Piano coda, identical with bar 3, and a written-out ritardando.

The deep, tonic-like bass notes with their harmonic 'strata' effect are remarkable in this song: E in the A sections, D and C sharp in the B sections, while the higher register characterizes the

Ex. 32

[1] International Society for Contemporary Music.

[2] To Willi Reich, 20 October 1939. This concert never took place owing to the war.

C section, as at *blumige Spiele*. How Webern develops by variations
—or varies by development—is shown in Ex. 32 on page 50.
In the quickly moving middle section the motif of wide intervals and the minor second relationship of D–C sharp

Ex. 33

Korn um Korn auf silberner Schale

provide the material: this is already presented in enlarged form
in bar 6.

Ex. 34   Op. 4, No. I, 6

Op. 4 No. 1 is a particularly significant example of Webern's
technique of keeping a whole song in a 'floating' state, avoiding
climactic effects and obscuring the rhythmic flow by syncopated
formations and a combination of triplets and duplets. The second
song is characteristic in its treatment of the voice as well as for its
solution of the problem of form. The text is in eight lines with
eleven syllables in each line. Webern therefore develops eight
melodic curves of eleven notes each, in which quavers predomi-
nate. Lengthening of rhythmic and intervallic elements occurs at
certain points in the text (*Duldens Schönheit, die späten Stunden*).
The lay-out in related phrases beginning with an up-beat is changed
in the fifth line, so that the word *nie* is given a strong declamatory
accent. At this point there is also a chromatic group of nine notes
closely crowded together, no doubt in order to concentrate the
expression as Ex. 35 shows:

Ex. 35

But the separate arcs of melody are also extremely chromatic in themselves:

Line of poem	Bar	Number of Melody Notes	Notes repeated	Number of different Chromatic notes
I	1–3	11	1	10
II	3–6	11	1	10
III	6–8	11	4	7
IV	8–10	11	1	10
V	11–13	11	3	8
VI	14–16	11	2	9
VII	16–18	11	2	9
VIII	18–20	11	2	9

It is remarkable that the poetic structure does not echo any kind of parallel in the musical construction. Tippett has said: 'What so fascinated the composers of the Schoenberg school about George was clearly not so much his masterly handling of words and his strict verse forms as his world of expression.'

The whole of Op. 4 shows how much the minor second is a principle of construction, dominating the building of chords as well as part-writing; this is especially clear in bar 4 of the second song, with its seven minor second interval tensions B–C–D flat –D natural–E flat–E natural–F:

Ex. 36   Op. 4, No. II, 4

The only motivic correspondence is in the piano coda, which overlaps with the last line of the voice part, and is an exact transposition of bars 6–8. The unaccompanied C in the coda attains the highest intensity through its complementary relationship to the chords surrounding it. With sounds arranged in this and similar ways people have often spoken of the 'harmony of fourths', and, referring to the penultimate chapter of Schoenberg's *Harmonielehre*, have seen the fourth as the structural interval. But in laying out minor second sounds in extended positions on the piano both fourths and sevenths (as a fourth plus a fourth) probably emerge by themselves, if construction by thirds and fifths is no longer a structural principle and the octave is ruled out as a doubling interval. In chords of this kind the fourth is of secondary importance.

The last song of Op. 4, *Ihr tratet zu dem Herde*, was Webern's first published work. It appeared in 1912 together with songs by Schoenberg and Berg in the *Blaue Reiter*, edited by Kandinsky and Marc, and introduced Webern to a small group of connoisseurs and interested amateurs; but it also established his position, as far as a wider public was concerned, in the increasingly bitter controversy which raged around Schoenberg and the New Music.

Five Movements for String Quartet, Op. 5 (1909)

I   *Heftig bewegt*
II *Sehr langsam*

III *Sehr bewegt*
IV *Sehr langsam*
 V *In zarter Bewegung*

Arranged for string orchestra by the composer, 1929.

> I am happy that my quartet made such an impression on you and Pepo. It is exactly a quarter of a century since I wrote it. As there have always been battles in connection with it right up to most recent times, I don't feel that this is such a long time ago. And only now can I myself really evaluate what I did at that time. And yet it seems to me that the other day I didn't listen in any different way from twenty-five years ago! (To Hildegard Jone, 9 November 1934.)

> Webern explained that the quartet pieces Op. 5 and probably also the Bagatelles Op. 9 were chosen from a large number of such creations. Because of his importance for the musical consciousness of the present day it is a most pressing duty to search out these unpublished works and publish them. (Theodor W. Adorno, *Klangfiguren*, p. 168.)

If one lets the string quartet movements make their effect on one quite simply, purely as sound, it becomes clear why after three vocal works Webern wrote only instrumental compositions in his Opp. 5–11 (with the exception of the Two Songs, Op. 8). The world of feeling released by George's poems led to visions of sound which were realized in the years between 1909 and 1914 in the medium of the string quartet (Opp. 5 and 9), the orchestra (Opp. 6 and 10) and solo instruments with piano (Opp. 7 and 11).

The so-called technical requirements for the players are not unusual, but extraordinary in sound effects: *sul ponticello* and *col legno*; quick changes from arco to pizzicato and back; dynamic contrasts in the shortest space; frequent passages in the extreme registers of sound and subtle 'hairpin dynamics', all of which demand complete mastery, especially of bowing.

For the mostly unprepared listener the pieces of Op. 5 present grave problems owing to their brevity; the length of the whole work is about eight minutes, as stated on the score; the third piece, the scherzo of the set, lasts thirty-five seconds! The listener has hardly begun to find his way in a few motivic and formal relationships when the piece comes to an end. The generation of 1910, which was accustomed, or gradually becoming accustomed, to the long symphonic periods of Wagner, Bruckner, Strauss, Reger and Mahler, must have been given a shock by Webern's Op. 5. The motivic concentration is so great that exact analysis is necessary to appreciate the various connections, as well as frequent hearings, so that the ear can grasp them. Křenek[1] says of the study of music of this kind: 'It was one of the most important experiences of my life that the patient, analytical and intellectual study of this music opened my eyes to its aesthetic value, and that as a result of my studies I am now in the position of being able to appreciate and immediately enjoy those beauties which were a closed book to me before I had studied this music analytically.'

In the first piece, a concisely constructed sonata movement, two minor-second motifs are presented with Beethovenian terseness and then concentrated into an f f f *col legno* chord.

Ex. 37

Op. 5, No. I, 1

The main motifs of the movement are developed further in the semiquaver movement of the two violins, which rapidly sinks to ppp.[2] As early as bar 7 the second subject begins, consisting of an antecedent in the cello and a consequent in both violins: the Viennese thirds and sixths of the latter remind one of the charms of *Rosenkavalier*—which was, however, not staged till 1911. Long

---

[1] *Selbstdarstellung*, p. 33.   [2] See Kolneder, *Klangtechnik*, p. 37 on this.

passages of the development section, which begins in bar 14, are
derived motivically from the antecedent.

Ex. 38

(heard as an inversion of the pizzicato
figure of bar 13 rather than, as Leibowitz says, a variation of the viola
thirds in bar 7)

The development ends with a ten-bar group (bars 27–36) which,
though developed from bars 12, 13, 7 and 1, has the effect of a new
development theme. In the recapitulation not only is the main
section by-passed, but also the individual elements of the second
subject are so strongly varied, partly by curtailment and partly by
expansion, that the recapitulation can hardly be appreciated as
such by the ear. A shortened form of the cello antecedent now
appears in the first violin, while viola and cello take over an
expanded form of the consequent, enriched by a counter-theme
in the first violin which is clearly derived from bars 2 and 3 but is
enlarged by the chief motif of the development theme. In contrapuntally combining the second subject with motifs from the main
theme, was Webern aiming at a condensation in time of the
recapitulation? The final section, from bar 44 on, is again dominated by the opening motif of the movement: an insertion, built
from the development theme (bar 49 = bars 34–35, bar 50 = bar

28) provides the climax of the movement with eight-part chords, each of them full of minor second relations and standing in a total 'leading note tension' to each other. The first chord is A–B flat, D sharp–E–F–F sharp, C–C sharp: the second chord E–F–F sharp–G–G sharp–A, B natural, D.[1]

Webern's techniques of sound are shown very characteristically at the beginning of the fourth movement.

Ex. 39

Op. 5, No. IV

The specific quality of the first chordal structures, which glimmer as if unreal, arises from their minor second structure—E–F, B–C: F–F sharp, B–C—in combination with the way they are to be played (muted, *sul ponticello*). The four-note motif which begins in bar 3, two 'arpeggiations' of chords of type Va,[2] is the horizontal projection of the chord in bar 2. This motif is taken over at the distance of a semitone by second violin and then cello, and all the entries in this example come at this interval, either together or a quaver later. And the little imitative passage between first violin and cello in bar 5 is also worked out at this interval, either in itself or in relation to the complementary part in the viola.

A further characteristic of these five string quartet pieces is the development of widely separated strata of sound either through held chords (especially in No. 2) or through pedal points with or without the splitting up of chords into ostinato figures, as in No. 4

[1] Compare also bars 5–6, H.S.   [2] See Ex. 16, p. 39.

from bar 7, No. 3 at the opening and from bar 15. The difference from Debussy's similar procedures lies in the fact that the melodic movement above the chords is in a minor-second relationship to them. Webern's Op. 5 marks an important stage in the approach to his world of sound, especially because the condensation of the language into the smallest possible space demands special concentration on the part of the listener. Schoenberg, in his *Harmonielehre* in the chapter 'Aesthetic Valuation of chords of six or more notes', quotes a bar from this Op. 5 (No. 1 bar 5) as an example. In conjunction with similar examples from his own works and others from Schreker, Bartók and Berg he goes on to say: 'Why this is so and why it is right I cannot say in detail at present. In general it appears natural to anyone who accepts my view of the nature of dissonance. But I believe firmly that it is right, and a number of others believe this too. It seems that the chromatic scale could be made responsible for the sequence of chords. The chords are mostly in such a relation that the second one contains as many notes as possible which are chromatic heightenings of the notes of the previous chord. But these rarely occur in the same part.'

Six Pieces for Orchestra, Op. 6 (1909)

To Arnold Schoenberg my teacher and friend in greatest affection

I	*Langsam*	0.55 min.	IV	*Sehr mässig*	3.15 min.
II	*Bewegt*	1.10 min.	V	*Sehr langsam*	1.50 min.
III	*Mässig*	0.50 min.	VI	*Langsam*	1.15 min.

Sound is the soul of form, which can only come alive through sound and works from the inside outwards. The form is the outer expression of the inner content. (Wassily Kandinsky, *Über die Formfrage*, 1912.)

Schoenberg's Five Orchestral Pieces, Op. 16, completed on 23 May 1909, with their often discussed experiments in the so-called 'melody of tone colour', provided the immediate impulse for Webern's Op. 6, which Wildgans dates 1910, and also for Alban Berg's Three Orchestral Pieces of 1914. The radical difference between the natures of the three composers, and in particular Webern's spiritual independence from his teacher, has often been pointed out, especially by W. Isensee, who has made a comparative study of the three works. While Berg is strongly indebted to Mahler's example, Schoenberg, in contrast to his own George song cycle Op. 15, written a year earlier, shows himself 'almost reactionary', especially by 're-adoption of definite motifs' and emphasis on organization in periods.

Webern's work can be regarded from two aspects. First of all he clearly wanted to expand the world of sound, presented in his Op. 5 through the string quartet, through the medium of a large orchestra. In the first version of 1909 he uses four each of flutes and oboes, five clarinets, three bassoons, six each of horns, trumpets and trombones and a tuba, in addition to the strings (in the revised version of 1928 the wind were reduced to 2.2.3.2. 4.4.4.1) and in addition harp, celesta, timpani and a lot of percussion —glockenspiel, cymbal, triangle, bass drum, side drum, tam-tam and bells without definite pitch. This provides a very rich palette of colours: but in comparison with the string quartet movements it seems that the richness of colour was if anything harmful to the intensity of expression. The instrumentation sought for here is shown in the treatment of lines as well as of chords. A melody at the beginning of the first piece is divided between three instruments.

Ex. 40

In the middle part in bars 4–7 of the same piece harp, solo viola and solo second violin take over from each other.

Ex. 41

The fourth piece was originally called *alla marcia funebre*, but this title does not appear in the printed score. Redlich[1] sees in

[1] *Berg*, p. 66.

this movement a 'musical echo' of Mahler's funeral service, but Mahler died at least a year after the piece was written. Willi Reich wrote about this funeral march in 1930: 'Over the hollow march rhythms of the brass and percussion tentative laments of the solo woodwind instruments are unfolded, which are stifled by a thunderous crescendo by the whole orchestra (minus strings!). It is impossible to imagine a more compelling impression of a funeral ceremony.'[1] At the beginning three chords alternate with the following instrumentation:

Ex. 42

2 Fl.   4 Hr.   4 Trp.
2 Clar. (con sord.) (con sord.)

This is clearly modelled on Schoenberg's Op. 16 No. 3, 'Colours'. (In his diary entry of 27 January 1912 Schoenberg calls the piece 'Chord colourings'; he invented the title after writing the piece, at the request of the publisher!) The seamless merging into each other of sounds of this kind demands a lot of work at rehearsal; Op. 6 is a ticklish orchestral work, although—or perhaps because —not much appears to 'happen' in it. Adorno has shown that even in the post-Wagnerian period 'in truly differentiated compositions unbroken melody for long periods is found less and less . . . even the individual melodies have dissolved into more and more refined elements. So the task in performance is to unite the differences, what has been separated by colour, and above all to close the leaps from one instrument or group of instruments to another.'[2]

Op. 6 has a striking tendency towards harmony in several different strata, showing impressionistic influences. Passages like bars 11–14 of No. 4, like the trombone chords in bars 19–29 of the same piece, are rarely found in Webern outside Op. 6.

The other aspect of these six orchestral pieces is their formal shape, in which they differ essentially from the works of Schoenberg and Berg mentioned above. Even in some of the Op. 5 pieces the aphoristic brevity, so typical of one creative period of

[1] *Die Musik*, 1930/813.   [2] *Klangfiguren*, p. 57.

Webern's, accompanied the abolition of motivic working. Looking back on this time Webern said in 1932: 'As we gradually gave up tonality, there came the idea: we don't want to repeat, something new must come all the time! It's obvious that this doesn't work, as it destroys comprehensibility.'[1] The short form and the avoidance of motivic working complement each other. It is difficult to decide which of these two was the leading tendency in Webern's work. Schoenberg's idea of continuous development, with almost complete avoidance of formal parallels which are brought about in the first place through common motivic material, was brought into being by Webern before his master created the model for the non-thematic miniature compositions of the last fifty years with his Six Little Piano Pieces Op. 19. On the problem of small forms in Webern Leibowitz says: 'It goes without saying that the origin of this special preoccupation should be looked for in the Six Little Piano Pieces Op. 19 of Schoenberg, in which we find for the first time a musical work which does without any repetitions and sequences.'[2] But Webern's Opp. 5 and 6 were written in 1909–10 and Schoenberg's Op. 19 in 1911, as Leibowitz himself states in the lists of works in his book. This mistake of Leibowitz has been repeated elsewhere. Zillig says of Schoenberg's Op. 19: 'For Schoenberg they mark a stage. His pupil Webern and the latter's followers, who form an important centre of gravity in the development of music today, have created a lifework and a complete artistic direction from them.'[3] On the other hand it ought first to be established whether Schoenberg's Three Pieces for Chamber Orchestra of 1910, discovered by Rufer among his posthumous papers and first performed in Berlin in 1957, were written *before* Webern's first short pieces.

In the first piece of Webern's Op. 6 it can be clearly seen how small melodic figures moving in a characteristic direction, or with a 'germ' interval, are very freely developed and varied. The starting-point is a motif from Ex. 40 (see Ex. 43, p. 62).

Webern's Orchestral Pieces Op. 6 were performed on 31 March 1913 in the large Musikvereinssaal in Vienna under Schoenberg's direction. The programme, which began with

[1] *Lectures*, p. 60.   [2] *Schoenberg*, p. 197.   [3] *Variationen*, p. 79.

Ex. 43

Webern's work, consisted of Schoenberg's Chamber Symphony, four songs with orchestra by Zemlinsky, Berg's songs with orchestra Op. 4 and Mahler's *Kindertotenlieder*. In his book on Berg, Redlich says:

> The concert could not be played through to the end because of the rude behaviour of a section of the audience. According to Wellesz's account of this concert one part of the audience had clearly come with the intention of provoking a scandal. General unrest already made itself felt during the individual pieces of Webern's Op. 6. In Berg's songs the noise was so great that one could hardly hear any of the music. . . . The concert ended early—that is without Mahler's *Kindertotenlieder*— in an unruly mêlée which later had a sequel in court.[1]

A newspaper report mentions Webern, but this time not as a 'psychographer of pianissimo dynamics': 'Herr von Webern'

[1] p. 60.

shouted from his box that the whole gang should be thrown out . . .'[1] About Webern's composition the same reporter wrote:

Immediately after the first section of the programme, an orchestral piece by Anton von Webern, the applauders and the hissers waged a battle for several minutes, but this remained within the limits more than sufficiently known to us from other Schoenberg performances. After the second orchestral piece a storm of laughter went through the hall, which was over-whelmed by the thunderous applause of the supporters of this nerve-shattering and provocative music. The remaining four pieces—the work consists of six short pieces without titles— also helped to create an atmosphere in the hall which made one fear the worst.

Four Pieces for Violin and Piano, Op. 7 (1910)

I   *Sehr langsam*
II *Rasch*
III *Sehr langsam*
IV *Bewegt*

'Music should not decorate, it should be truthful.' (Schoenberg, *Probleme des Kunstunterrichts*, 1911.)

Opp. 1–8 were written in the space of only three years. Webern must have been in an almost feverish state of creative pressure at the time; after a masterpiece in the traditional style came the liberation from tradition, the finding of his personality in the new sphere of sonorities and testing out of all the new adventures in sound. The Violin Pieces Op. 7 are especially characteristic of this stage of his search. The brevity of language (which its denigrators called 'form-shrinking') is carried still further; No. 1 is 9 bars long, No. 2 24 bars, No. 3 14 and No. 4 15 bars, and motivic parallels are almost entirely lacking. As in some passages in Op. 6 there are again widespread 'strata' of sound. These con-trast with Webern's endeavour, noticeable from Op. 2 onward, to contract the course of the harmonies through colour effects into a narrow space. The fact that these 'strata-effects' often use

[1] Quoted in the Schoenberg number of the *Anbruch*, 1924.

an ostinato technique seems to imply a further contradiction of
the principle of avoiding repetition. Webern was naturally very
well acquainted with Debussy's methods of harmonic strata-
construction and clearly used them consciously as a structural
element: tonality and thematic elements were being avoided to
a great extent. Bars 6–9 of the third piece are characteristic of his
method of working.

Ex. 44
Op. 7, No. III, 5·

The chromatic seven-note melody in the upper part of the piano
is supported by a pedal point and a chromatic eight-note ostinato
on the violin. Similar passages can be found in Op. 7 No. 1
bars 6–9, and No. 2 bars 1–2, 9–11 and 18. From the technical
point of view Op. 7 seems to be even more strongly built on
minor second relationships than the earlier works: e.g. the beginning of No. 3 or bars 9–11 of the same piece (Ex. 44). Over a
chordal sound of Type I (see p. 39) a two-note motif is heard
which expands the total sound up to G sharp–A–A sharp–B–C.
The marking 'hardly audible' (but with accent) is characteristic.
Peter Stadlen, who studied Webern's Piano Variations with the
composer and gave the first performance of them, tells us how

literally Webern wanted to have indications of this kind interpreted. For sounds which existed almost more 'in the head' than in performance, Webern, according to a joke made by his friends, invented the term 'pensato'—'thought of'.

As well as a ppp-piece like No. 3, Op. 7 also contains outbreaks in ff and fff, mostly combined with wide intervals and extreme dynamic values in quick succession.

Ex. 45
Op. 7, No. IV, 1

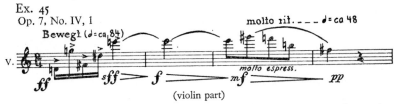

(violin part)

These are essential characteristics of the expressionist style, and in Webern's next creative period they appear more and more, and above all in a concentration which does cause special problems for the listener. Connected with this is 'rubato performance' which Webern often indicated by exact markings. In No. 2, in 24 bars of moderate tempo the following tempo alterations are asked for: Quick (crotchet = 112)—rit.—Broad (crotchet = ca 72)—Tempo I (crotchet = 112)—rit.—Slower (crotchet = ca 72)—Slow (crotchet = 48)—rit.—Tempo I (crotchet = 112)—rit.—Slower (crotchet = ca 72)—accel.—Tempo I—molto rit. —crotchet = ca 48—Tempo I.

Bars 10–13 of No. 4 provide an example of chromatic groups, formation of motifs from types of chordal sounds and dovetailed seconds.

Ex. 46
Op. 7, No. IV, 9

After a six-note group A–B flat, D–E flat, F sharp–G, we hear C sharp and G sharp which are in a complementary relationship to it. The motif in the upper part of the piano has a double minor-second relationship to this. The line drawn in the example shows a ten-note group. The chromatic seven-note violin figure, typical in shape, is complementary to the bass note in the piano part.

Two Songs on poems by Rainer Maria Rilke Op. 8, for voice, clarinet (also bass clarinet), horn, trumpet, celesta, harp, violin, viola and cello (1910)

I   *Du, der ichs nicht sage*
II *Du machst mich allein*

... now you should not conclude from this that I meant ... that it wouldn't matter what 'text' one chose: I think I have proved the contrary during the whole of my life. (Webern to Hildegard Jone, 8 August 1934.)

After the George settings of Opp. 2–4 Webern turned to Rilke. The choice of text is characteristic of the shy, sensitive, introvert man, whose life was not fulfilment but renunciation:

> You whom I do not tell
> That at night
> I lie weeping,
> whose being makes me sleepy,
> like a cradle:
> You who do not tell me
> when she is awake because of me:
> How if we were to endure
> this glory
> without remaining silent?
> Behold the lovers:
> once they begin to confess,
> how soon they lie.

On his path towards an increasing differentiation of sounds it was natural for Webern to use a chamber ensemble instead of the piano when after three instrumental works he again began to set texts. The instruments of his small ensemble are very sparingly used. In the first song the trumpet has nine notes to play, and the viola enters four times with double stops and a harmonic. The instruments often have only a rhythmical function, rather like chords in accompanied recitative. Melodically they chiefly appear in little clusters of notes, to bridge rests or long-held notes in the voice part. There are two-, three- and four-note projections of the chord-types we have met before and further developments of characteristic motifs from the voice part:

Ex. 47

The voice dominates in long melodic lines, which are completely conditioned by the meaning of the text. The next example shows Webern's relationship to words at this stage. High notes and expansions are found in exactly the places in which they come in natural speech. Webern's use of the vocal line in wide intervals is based on this declamation, which follows the sense of the text without rhetoric or sentimentality.

Ex. 48

Craft, in his introduction to the recording, suggests singing

Webern's voice parts, not merely reading or listening to them, in order to understand their character. One can only agree with him, and those who have traced in actual song the masterly declamation of passages like the one above will perhaps find the key to the most problematic side of Webern's technique of composition: his use of the voice in the works of his middle period.

THE INSTRUMENTAL MINIATURES

Six Bagatelles for String Quartet, Op. 9 (1913)

I	*Mässig*	30 secs.	IV	*Sehr langsam*	35 secs.
II	*Leicht bewegt*	21 secs.	V	*Äusserst langsam*	1·10 min.
III	*Ziemlich fliessend*	16 secs.	VI	*Fliessend*	17 secs.

His language, with all its greatest intensity, is simple, often noticeably shy and suppressed: the most soul-shattering experiences are hinted at in a few words. (J. Polnauer on Webern's literary style, Preface to the Letters to Hildegard Jone and Josef Humplik.)

When the Bagatelles were printed in 1924 Schoenberg wrote the following introduction to them:

Though the brevity of these pieces is a persuasive advocate for them: on the other hand this very brevity needs an advocate. One has to realize what restraint it needs to express oneself with such brevity. Every glance can be expanded into a poem, every sigh into a novel. But to express a novel in a single gesture, joy in a single breath: such concentration can only be found where self-pity is lacking in equal measure.

These pieces can only be understood by those who believe that sound can say things which can only be expressed through sound.

They stand up to criticism as little as beliefs of any kind.

If faith can move mountains, unbelief can deny their existence. Against such impotence faith is impotent.

Does the player now know how he should perform these pieces, or the listener how he should take them in? Can believing players and listeners fail to surrender themselves to each other?

But what should one do with the heathen? Fire and sword can keep them quiet: but only believers need to be restrained.

May this silence sound for them!

The apostolic character and the sophistication of this 'recommendation' have been attacked, not without reason. But Schoenberg's words should be understood from the situation of the time. In the conditions of creative work at that time Webern's miniatures must have appeared as mere remote products of a wilful aesthetic which really needed a powerful plea. Webern dedicated the pieces to Alban Berg (though not in the score), and in the dedication he has provided the key to all his later works: 'Multum non multa. How happy I would be if this phrase could apply here.' In 1913–14 Webern carried the idea of the most concentrated musical language to its final stage in his instrumental works, Opp. 9–11. With this went a shrinking of the melodic material, which can occasionally be seen in the earlier works too, but marks a radical change from the Songs Op. 8. Two- and three-note motifs, mostly projections of sounds built up of minor seconds, are the rule here. The first Bagatelle is characteristic of the way in which they are constantly developed further. At the beginning a chord, C sharp–D–E flat (Type I) is presented in subtle colours, followed by a three-note motif in the second violin, C sharp–C. This is already the end of the 'exposition'. All the motivic shapes in the movement can be derived from the motivic material presented here and the falling movement of the cello in bars 2–3.

Ex. 49

In Op. 9 the two contrasted formative principles of twelve-note writing and the use of harmonic strata-formations also appear closely together, but the 'strata' are shorter than in Opp. 5–7 because of the brevity of the form.

At the beginning of No. 1 there is a twelve-note group (including the G of the first violin in bar 3), as well as in the first bars of No. 3. In the works up to Op. 17 twelve-note groups mostly come at the beginning or at especially marked formal divisions. This may be owing to the tendency to lead the listener right at the beginning into the expressive world of sounds of great tension, at a moment when the ear is perhaps especially sensitive to repetitions of notes. This is a really 'heard', not a constructed kind of twelve-note writing. ('Listen profoundly' was one of Berg's favourite dictums in his teaching!) In a lecture Webern said: 'Some remarkable things were involved in this—they didn't arise from theory but from listening. Thus it proved disturbing if a note was repeated within a theme.'[1] And it is clear from another passage in the lectures that the very advanced twelve-note writing in Op. 9 did not come by chance, but that total chromaticism (without serial technique!) was consciously aimed at: 'I can tell you something from my own experience: about 1911 I wrote the Bagatelles for string quartet, Op. 9, all very short pieces, lasting two minutes; perhaps the shortest there have been in music up to now. Here I had the feeling that when the twelve notes have all been played the piece is over. Much later I realized that all this was a part of necessary development. In my sketchbook I wrote out the chromatic scale and crossed off individual notes. Why? Because I had convinced myself that the note was already there. It sounds grotesque, incomprehensible, and it was incredibly difficult. The inner ear decided absolutely rightly that the person who had written out the chromatic scale and crossed off individual notes *was no fool*. (Josef Matthias Hauer also experienced and discovered all this in his own way.) In short, a law came into being. Until all twelve notes have appeared none of them must appear again. . . . We were not then conscious of the principle but had been sensing it for a long time.'[2]

Harmonic 'strata-effects' occur in the fourth Bagatelle: over the subtly arranged sound F sharp–G, C sharp–D the first violin plays a melody in harmonics which is harmonically complementary.

[1] *Lectures*, p. 42.   [2] *Lectures*, p. 51.

Ex. 50

Op. 9, No. IV, 5

At the beginning of this piece there is again a twelve-note group, made up of harmonically complementary motifs in close minor-second relationships, and with indications of a 'strata-effect' in the first violin. As in Ex. 50 the 'strata-technique' is combined with chromatic twelve-note organization in the writing.

But the most astonishing piece is Op. 9 in Bagatelle No. 5, of which Pousseur has made a comprehensive study.[1] The motivic material is reduced to a minimum, and with pp as the highest dynamic, and with the most refined methods of playing technique, sounds are produced which represent the actual structural element, the construction being entirely based on minor seconds, sounded together or separately.

Ex. 51

Op. 9, No. V, 1

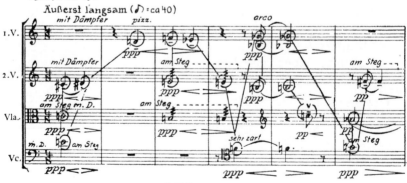

[1] *Reihe*, 2/51.

To understand pieces of this kind it is necessary to hear these sounds not as notes added to one another but as unities: this can be done by frequent hearings. The electronic musicians have asserted that Webern advanced into regions of sound the realization of which belongs to electronic resources. With this they have made him, somewhat too hastily, into the ancestor of electronic composition.

It is interesting to see in this style how disturbing a consonance sounds which occurs by mistake: on the record the viola player has made an error of clef in bar 6—instead of the minor second G–A flat we hear the 'wrong' major-sixth B flat–G.

Five Pieces for Orchestra, Op. 10 (1911–13)

I	*Sehr ruhig and zart*	Original form	12 bars	28 secs.
II	*Lebhaft und zart bewegt*	Change	14 bars	14 secs.
III	*Sehr langsam und äusserst ruhig*	Return	11 bars	1.45 min.
IV	*Fliessend, äusserst zart*	Remembrance	6 bars	19 secs.
V	*Sehr fliessend*	Soul	32 bars	47 secs.

In considering atonal music it is very confusing that in deciding what is satisfactory and what are the harmonic results of the counterpoint one possesses no definite points to hold on to, no 'rules'. In this respect both the composers and their audiences have to rely only on their instinct. (Béla Bartók, *The Problem of Modern Music*, 1920.)

The titles used at the first performance in Vienna, which are not in the score, have been handed down by Willi Reich, who says that the composer 'did not wish to give any programmatic explanation by them, but only to indicate the feelings which ruled him while composing the different pieces'.[1]

The key to the understanding of these pieces, which 'have already ended before they have begun', or 'of which Webern has only written the coda', as it has been maliciously said, can perhaps be obtained from the instrumentation, which is clearly divided into three groups:

[1] *Die Musik*, 1930/814.

I   Four strings: solo violin, solo viola, solo cello, solo double-bass.

II   A wind group: flute (also piccolo), oboe, clarinet in B flat (also bass clarinet in B flat), clarinet in E flat, horn in F, trumpet in B flat, trombone.

III   A group of 'colour instruments': harmonium, celesta, mandolin, guitar, harp, percussion (glockenspiel, xylophone, cow bells, deep bells, triangle, cymbals, side drum, bass drum).

It may be surprising to see the percussion instruments included in the last group, but for Webern they are not rhythmical instruments in this work but chiefly instruments of colour—as for Bartók later in his sonata for two pianos and percussion. The remaining instruments in this group are used in a similar way. The use of all this rich variety of colour is very sparing: the complete seven wind instruments only play in No. 2, and then never at the same time; four of them play in No. 1 and three in No. 3. The guitar is only used in Nos. 3 and 5: the harmonium is silent in two of the pieces and has only two two-part chords to play in No. 3; in No. 4 the percussion is not used at all, apart from three ppp strokes on the side drum. This instrumentation, like a whispered breath, corresponds to the character of the pieces, of which three take place in pp–ppp dynamics.

No. 3 shows how these instrumental groups are used to build form. The piece is in three sections:

A   6/4 time   Bars 1–4   *Sehr langsam und äusserst ruhig;*
B   3/4, 2/4 time   5–6   *Drängend, zögernd—molto rit.;*
A₁ 6/4 time   7–11   *Tempo*

In the first three bars mandolin, guitar, celesta and harp create a glimmering web of sound on the notes G sharp–A–B flat and C sharp–D–E, supported by bells and cow bells without definite pitch, 'hardly audible—fading away'. There is a similar web in the return of the A-section (C sharp–D–D sharp–E–F) on cello (muted, harmonic), harp, celesta, mandolin and harmonium, also coloured by a roll on the percussion instruments. 'Wrapped' in these sounds the melody instruments play four-note motifs.

The two-bar middle section provides a contrast, in which the lively clarinet melody has a three-note counterpoint on guitar and cello pizzicato in unison. The melodic kernel of the piece— —basic motifs in free development—is given to strings and wind.

Ex. 52

Referring to Op. 10 Leibowitz and all those who have copied him without studying the score have laid a one-sided emphasis on the 'melody of tone colour'. This concept, of which Stravinsky said[1] that it needed a definition, as it had acquired so many meanings, was described by Schoenberg on the last page of his *Harmonielehre*: 'I cannot draw an unconditional distinction between sound colour and sound pitch, as it is usually expressed. I find that the note makes itself heard through the sound colour, of which the sound pitch is a dimension. So the colour is the large area, the pitch is a part of it. The pitch is in fact the colour measured in a certain direction. If it is possible to create from colours differing in pitch structures which we call melodies, sequences of sounds which create an effect similar to thoughts when connected together, then it must also be possible to create similar sequences out of what we call tone colour of the other dimensions, out of what we call tone-colour for want of a better name, sequences whose relations to each other work with a kind of logic which is equivalent to that logic which is sufficient for us in a melody of sound pitches. This seems to be a fantasy of the future and probably is so too. But one which I firmly believe will happen. . . . Melodies of tone colour! What refined senses can make distinctions here, what a highly developed spirit to find pleasure in such subtle things!'

[1] *Melos*, 1958/169.

Here Leibowitz joins in: 'Such a projection towards the future could only stimulate the spirit of Webern: in fact the idea of the melody of tone colour obsessed him throughout his whole career ... the first piece of Op. 10 is the one where the striving for melody of tone colour is strongly marked.'[1] Karkoschka attacked this point of view in a fundamental manner.[2] If in the fifth piece, bar 18, Webern adds to a unison motif of the celesta and harp (Type IIIa) a string harmonic on each note, he is merely using an artistic device which was already well known in the impressionistic orchestration of 1910. And in the often quoted beginning of No. 1 the harp motif B–C–B merely acquires additional colours from other instruments:

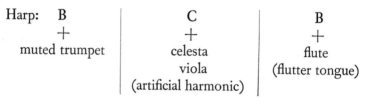

Harp: B	C	B
+	+	+
muted trumpet	celesta viola (artificial harmonic)	flute (flutter tongue)

And if the final bar of the piece

Ex. 53

is described as: 'The coda shows a melody of tone colour on the F,'[3] then one must point out that this kind of thing was well known to Vivaldi 200 years earlier.[4]

What is much more striking in Op. 10 is the high state of chromatic penetration in the writing. At the beginning of No. 2, E flat clarinet and solo violin complement each other contrapuntally in an eleven-note group:

---

[1] *Schoenberg*, p. 199. [2] *Zur Entwicklung*, p. 125. [3] Leibowitz, *Schoenberg*, p. 202. [4] Kolneder, *Aufführungspraxis bei Vivaldi*, p. 115.

Ex. 54

The missing E flat is in the subsidiary trumpet part. In No. 3, discussed above, the motifs which are heard above the 'webs' are complementary to them. In the final section this produces a nine-note group, and at the beginning a twelve-note one, if one includes the final notes E flat in the horn and G in the cello. In No. 5, as in No. 4, two twelve-note groups appear in the first four bars, here joined by a common C. One can only agree with Leibowitz' view of Op. 10: 'Listening to this music plunges the unprepared listener into total confusion, which can only be overcome by long acclimatization.'[1] What shocks the listener so much at the first contact is not only the brevity of these pieces, but their apparent lack of content. From the point of view current in 1927 Mersmann saw the end of music in this very work. He speaks of a 'process of decomposition which threatens Webern' and says about him:

> ... he shows the whole danger of the state of development provided by Schoenberg's works. Webern too writes 'pieces' for violin and piano, for string quartet or for orchestra. If in Schoenberg this form means the highest degree of concentration and thus of the most intense activity, in Webern the same procedure slips into a state of passivity. Development, shape, the urge to construct has long disappeared from his music. It is deeply tired: it cannot form anything, it can scarcely even breathe any more. I reproduce here the fourth of his Five Pieces for Orchestra Op. 10 [musical example]. These six bars are a 'piece'. Here and there a scanty, refined, desiccated chord, a few figures blown away by mandolin, trumpet and violin, detached, isolated single notes—that is all. The score, for

[1] *Schoenberg*, p. 202.

eleven instruments, looks like a parody. The dynamics go from piano downwards to triple pianissimo. If one came across this music without knowing from what background or milieu it came one would take it for the work of a joker, some little composition student who wanted to make fun of modern music. There is nothing to divide it objectively from that except the name of the composer on the score. Here is the end of a road. We have reached the end of music, the absolute final point.'[1]

Vis-à-vis the author of these remarks one has to admit the fact that Webern himself did not pursue this kind of development any further.

Webern's orchestral works have now become 'balletic': the New York City Ballet put on a ballet called *Episodes* to orchestral works of Webern's, with choreography by George Balanchine and Martha Graham.[2]

Three Little Pieces for Cello and Piano, Op. 11 (1914)

I	*Mässige Achtel* (ca 58)	9 bars	53 secs.
II	*Sehr bewegt* (crotchet = ca 160)	13 bars	13 secs.
III	*Äusserst ruhig* (quaver = ca 50)	10 bars	45 secs.

Webern can say more in two minutes than most other composers in ten. (Humphrey Searle, *Twentieth Century Counterpoint*, p. 104.)

The cello pieces mark an extreme point of development among the miniature instrumental pieces, and not only because of their brevity. The conciseness of the melodic writing is brought to a stage here which is not found again till late Webern. These little pieces are woven out of two-, three- and four-note motifs whose interrelations can only be grasped after repeated hearings and in good performances.

In the first piece Webern has indicated a division into four sections by his typical tempo markings 'rit. . . . Tempo'. The first section begins with a 'one-note' motif and a chord of five notes which together make up a six-note group with three semitonal

---

[1] *Moderne Musik*, p. 144.   [2] *Neue Zeitschrift für Musik*, 1959/484.

78

intervals in it: the four-note motif in the piano, whose leap of a tenth is answered by the cello, is supported by a complementary chord. By overlapping into the second section, which is developed in a similar way, a twelve-note group appears. Complementary chromaticism also dominates the rest of the piece: in bar 7 there is a nine-note group, the last two bars contain an eight-note group with one note repeated, and in the second and third sections of the piece an eleven-note and a twelve-note group overlap. Motivic relationships are chiefly audible in the way the phrases move:

Ex. 55

One ought to look at the second piece before speaking too lightly of 'pp Webern'. The dynamic markings there are as follows:

p	2x	ff	3x	sf	1x
mf	1x	fff	2x	sff	2x
f	10x	sfp	1x	sfff	1x

The first three bars are typical of Webern's motivic technique at this stage of development (see Ex. 56, p. 84). A twelve-note group is marked by the line: it appears through the combination of four three-note motifs built in his well-known way (see p. 39).

There immediately follow a nine-, a twelve- and a ten-note group and in the last two bars there is another ten-note group.

But the most astonishing piece from the point of view of through-and-through chromaticism is No. 3: an eleven-note group (lasting as far as G in bar 5) is joined to a twelve-note group, with G and G sharp as their common notes. This piece was written almost nine years before the official discovery of the twelve-note method, and, after the twelve-note experiments in Op. 9, it is certainly one of the earliest, if not the first work of twelve-note music. It would be worth finding out if the line of development of Schoenberg's method, which, as is well known, links twelve-note writing to serial technique, is really Webern–Hauer–Schoenberg, and not, as generally supposed, Hauer–Schoenberg–Webern. In any case the latter does not use twelve-tone writing in a doctrinaire manner: at this stage it is one means of concentration of expression for him, among others. It is significant that it is often to be found at the beginning, but more rarely later on in a piece. Compare Leibowitz' statement: 'Webern's Op. 17 is his first twelve-note work. This may be his very first experience of the new technique.'[1] And Vlad says: 'When one goes on to consider the works of Berg and Webern which belong to this phase of the development of the twelve-note technique, one observes that there is no partially twelve-note work of Webern's.'[2]

It is also interesting that Webern was conscious throughout of the strongly experimental character of Op. 11. On 20 October 1939, in a letter to Willi Reich, he suggested songs from Opp. 2, 4 and 12 for a concert which was being planned in Basle and then said: 'As regards my instrumental works: if there were a *quartet* which, if it couldn't play all five pieces of Op. 5 but at any rate Nos. 2, 4 and 5 from it—that would be all right! and good! Otherwise the violin pieces would be better than the cello pieces. Definitely not those! Not that I don't think them good. But they would be entirely misunderstood. The players and the audience would find it hard to make anything of them. Nothing experimental!!!'

[1] *Introduction*, p. 86.   [2] *Storia*, p. 39.

THE SONGS OPP. 12–15

Four Songs for Voice and Piano, Op. 12

I   *Der Tag ist vergangen* (Folk song)
II   *Die geheimnisvolle Flöte* (Li-Tai-Po, from Hans Bethge's *Chinesische Flöte*)
III   *Schien mir's, als ich sah die Sonne* (from August Strindberg's *Ghost Sonata*)
IV   *Gleich und gleich* (Goethe)

Four Songs for Voice and Orchestra, Op. 13

Dedicated to Dr Norbert Schwarzmann[1].

I   *Wiese im Park* (Karl Kraus)
    13 solo instruments: flute, clarinet, bass clarinet, horn, trumpet, trombone, celesta, harp, glockenspiel, violin, viola, cello and double bass.
II   *Die Einsame* (Wang-Seng-Yu, from the *Chinesische Flöte*). Instrumentation as in I, with piccolo instead of flute.
III   *In der Fremde* (Li-Tai-Po, from the *Chinesische Flöte*)
    9 solo instruments: piccolo, clarinet, bass clarinet, trumpet, celesta, harp, violin, viola and cello.
IV   *Ein Winterabend* (Georg Trakl)
    10 solo instruments: clarinet, bass clarinet, trumpet, trombone, celesta, harp, violin, viola, cello and double bass.

Six Songs on poems of Georg Trakl, Op. 14 for voice, clarinet, bass clarinet, violin and cello

I   *Die Sonne (Täglich kommt die gelbe Sonne über den Hügel)*
II   *Abendland I (Mond, als träte ein Totes aus blauer Höhle)*
III   *Abendland II (So leise sind die grünen Wälder unsrer Heimat)*
IV   *Abendland III (Ihr grossen Städte steinern aufgebaut in der Ebene)*
V   *Nachts (Die Bläue meiner Augen ist erloschen im dieser Nacht)*
VI   *Gesang einer gefangenen Amsel (Dunkler Odem im grünen Gezweig)*

[1] Viennese neurologist, patron of Schoenberg, Berg and Webern. Schoenberg's Serenade Op. 24 was performed for the first time at his flat in 1924.

Five Sacred Songs, Op. 15 for voice, flute, clarinet (also bass
clarinet), trumpet, harp and violin (also viola)

I   *Das Kreuz, das musst' er tragen*
II   *Morgenlied* (from *Des Knaben Wunderhorn*)
III *In Gottes Namen aufstehen*
IV   *Mein Weg geht jetzt vorüber, o Welt*
V   *Fahr hin, o Seel', zu deinem Gott*

A song of yours is a bringer of joy to me, a bringer of joy which irradiates
my whole being. As when on dull days the sun suddenly breaks through
and one doesn't know why one is suddenly happy. It is just the same with
the scent of flowers. . . . (Alban Berg to Webern on 12 October 1925
regarding Webern's Op. 12.)

I am very pleased that you have mentioned my Trakl songs in this
connection. . . . But, between ourselves, it is hardly possible to make them
come off: I don't know a singer, and if I did there is not enough time. My
Trakl songs are pretty well the most difficult there are in this field. They
would need countless rehearsals. When could I do all this? I haven't a
possibility of doing it now. Yes, it's not so simple. Before there can be a
performance of a work of mine there have to be many, many given conditions and these are simply not there in our case. . . . (To Josef Humplik,
30 December 1929.)

The method so far used in this book, of studying Webern's works
one by one in order to penetrate the growth of his style, has been
useful up to now. But in the group of works which follows the
opus numbers do not correspond with the order of composition.
The songs in one opus were sometimes written as much as four
or five years apart, and the groups of songs overlap. Webern
clearly wrote these songs separately, without thinking of putting
them into groups, a procedure which came gradually later. In
Opp. 12 and 13 the combination of instruments makes the
common bond, even if the texts of Op. 13 are linked to each
other in content. Webern's fruitful settings of Trakl began with
Op. 14/IV. But it is remarkable that one song, *Ein Winterabend*,
written a year later, was not included in the Trakl song-cycle.
Here again it may have been the combination of instruments
which dictated the order. Finally, the texts of Op. 15 are folk
songs. The dates of composition and the overlapping of the
individual *opera* are shown in the following table:

1914	13/II
1915	12/I, 12/III
1916	12/II, 12/IV, 13/I, 13/III,14/IV, 15/V
1918	13/IV
1919	14/II, 14/III, 14/V, 14/VI
1921	14/I, 15/I, 15/III
1922	15/II, 15/IV

It is not easy to see unified tendencies of development in this group of works. The opinion, often expressed in similar form, that Webern's characteristic development was like a straight line can hardly be maintained if one compares Op. 11 No. 2 with Op. 12 No. 1.

Both works were written within a year of each other. But what a contrast! To an apostle of 'progress' Op. 12 must appear as a regression, a falling back into a stage of composition which had already been passed by and had now become a historical one. Op. 11 No. 2 shows a certain 'atomization' of the melodic line, but in Op. 12 long arcs of melody appear again, reaching back to the style of the Songs Op. 8. Is the difference to be explained by that between instrumental and vocal music, which is so clearly shown in the late works? Partly, but it is remarkable that Webern turned exclusively to compositions based on words for a long period: between 1915 and 1927, i.e. twelve years altogether, he wrote nothing but vocal works. It seems that Webern viewed the logical development which could have come from Opp. 9–11 with a kind of horror. Just as at a certain stage of his development Schoenberg saw the texts as first of all a useful skeleton in place of the structural powers of tonality which had now disappeared, Webern too, from 1914 on, saw the possibility of creating larger forms through the link with words. Op. 13 contains two songs each of five minutes' length: each of these songs is therefore almost as long as Opp. 9 and 11 together. 'With the Songs Op. 12 an almost unnoticeable change begins,' says Adorno.[1] 'Webern's music secretly expands: in his own way he is mastering the solution which Schoenberg first displayed in

[1] *Klangfiguren*, p. 171.

Ex. 56

Op. 11, No. II

Op. 12, No. I

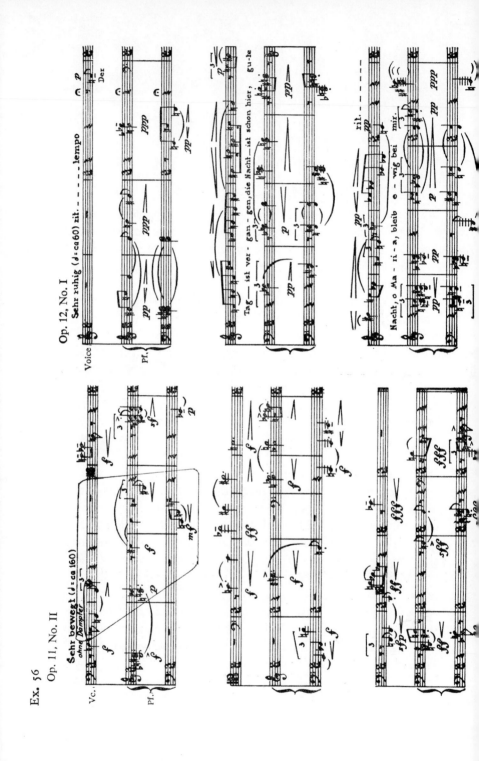

Pierrot Lunaire and the Songs Op. 22: that one cannot persist with the method of absolute purity without music being spiritually reduced to physical deterioration. The new expansion is only hinted at; the first and last of the songs are still aphoristically short, but they do breathe a little, and the two middle songs have well developed vocal lines, though certainly of a subtle character in which the earlier process of splitting-up is still maintained.'

The use of the voice in long phrases in Op. 12 No. 1 could be due to the characteristics of a folk text, but these long arcs are also found in the setting of the Strindberg poem (Op. 12 No. 3). The very early Op. 13 No. 2 shows how Webern's characteristic use of intervals arises solely out of the expressionistic, intensified interpretation of the words:

Ex. 57

Op. 13, No. II, 25

This kind of declamation coming from the text, leads more and more in the direction of a kind of Hoquet technique, which Webern as a musicologist certainly knew in musical history.

Ex. 58

Op. 15, No. I, 1

The last two bars of this song as well as other passages such as Op. 14/IV, bars 17–18 and Op. 14/VI, bars 10–14, are shaped in a similar way. In connection with this the melody is often split up into small motifs of the highest tension divided by rests, a technique of melodic writing which alternates with long melodic

lines at points of climax. Op. 15 No. 2 shows this treatment of
the vocal line. In the group of works Opp. 12–15 the melodic
handling of the voice shows more and more of instrumental
characteristics. As in Bach, where the high baroque method of
expression was realized more intensively in instrumental writing
than in vocal and was then taken over into sung parts, in Webern
wide intervals appear as a result of an expressive tension which
goes beyond the normal limits and appears especially strongly in
instrumental music, e.g. Opp. 5, 7 and 11; it has developed vocal
writing from within to the very limits of the possible. A passage
like the beginning of Op. 15 No. 2 shows this stage:

Ex. 59

Op. 15, No. II

Siehi auf, ihr lie - ben Kinderlein, der Mor - gen-stern.

Treated in isolation, such a use of the singing voice must seem
like the musical utterance of a madman. From the point of view
of Webern's development Op. 15 is the work which marks a
decisive point in an increasingly expressive concentration of the
writing which reaches its climax in the *String Trio*, Op. 20, there-
after to break off in a precipitous turning-point—again not at all
in a straight line. Beginning with some of the songs of Op. 13,
the instrumental interest clearly increases: through the overlapping of motifs, mostly consisting of only a few notes with
wide intervals, the writing is concentrated to an extreme degree,
which makes it extraordinarily difficult to take in this music.
Voice and instruments have become so equally balanced that the
listener is hardly helped by following the text in the voice part.
In addition simultaneous wide leaps in various parts, in opposite
directions as well, produce a perpetual crossing of parts, so
that it is almost impossible to listen to the individual lines. In
Op. 15 No. 2 there appears this violin part, in counterpoint to
the voice, which could come from a violin concerto or a solo
sonata:

Ex. 60

Op. 15, No. II

In addition there is a trumpet part in which there are thirty-six sevenths and larger intervals, mostly diminished or augmented, and only six seconds and eight thirds. The third instrument in the song, the bass clarinet, is handled in a similar way. Such a sound-language cannot be realized on the piano: thus after Op. 12 the piano is replaced by instrumental combinations, and Webern only returned to it in his late works. The giving up of and return to the piano took place in a symmetrical way:

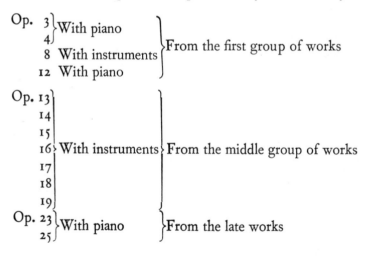

A comparison of the two songs, Op. 12 No. 1 (Ex. 56) and Op. 14 No. 4, written only two years apart, shows the path of Webern's development in the condensation of the writing.

87

Ex. 61

In his time Mersmann saw in the vocal style of Webern's music 'the last continuation of the impressionistic process of the dissolution of all links'.[1] But just in Op. 15 itself it is highly intensified expressionism and yet it clarified itself, when its spiritual conditions had altered.

The motivic concentration closely corresponds to the chromaticization, which is shown in the formation of complete or practically complete twelve-note groups. Thus Op. 12 No. 4 begins with a twelve-note group, and there is another from the second half of bar 7 onwards, while in the twelve-note group at the beginning of Op. 12 No. 1 (Ex. 56) a thrice-repeated G sharp is reminiscent of impressionistic 'strata-formations'.[2] The examples could be increased almost as much as one wished by including ten- and eleven-note groups.

Another stylistic trait of Webern's, which can be seen in the Songs Opp. 12–15, and which becomes more evident in the Canons Op. 16, is the tendency towards strict polyphonic treatment of the parts. This appears to be in contrast with the expressionistic over-intensification of works like Opp. 14 and 15 and ought probably to be understood as an attempt to control the internal forces bursting for expression. Passages like bars 4–12 in Op. 12 No. 4 have the effect of a three-part invention, especially because of the equal status of the parts; similarly in Op. 14 No. 4 (Ex. 61). This tendency led to Op. 15 No. 5 in 1917, which Webern subtitled in brackets 'Double canon in motu contrario', a predecessor of the 'Five Canons on Latin Texts' written seven years later and at the same time looking back to Op. 2. The voice part, which is almost simple in comparison with that of the remaining songs of Op. 15, is imitated in contrary motion at the interval of a bar and accompanied by imitative instrumental counterpoint in contrary motion as in Example 62:

[1] *Moderne Musik*, p. 144.
[2] Further complete chromatic groups are pointed out in Kolneder, *Klangtechnik*, p. 44.

Ex. 62

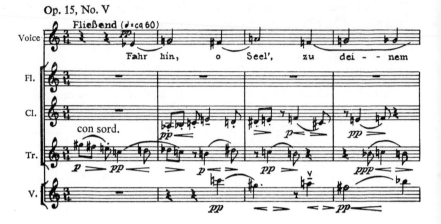

Op. 15, No. V

Through differences in articulation, and also through instrumental effects which are impossible on the imitating instruments, e.g. flute flutter-tongue, violin and harp pizzicato, Webern attempts to give each part a certain independence apart from the imitation. For a double canon structure voice and three instruments would have been enough, but Webern uses flute, clarinet, trumpet (always muted), harp (used as a single-part melody instrument) and violin. The two apparently superfluous instruments make it possible to divide up the part which is imitating the vocal line into sections, which not only increases the richness of the colour but also enables the instrumentation to underline the formal divisions of the first verse, while in the second the entries of the different colours are even more split up:

Voice	*Imitation*
Fahr hin, o Seel', zu deinem Gott	Violin
der dich aus nichts gestaltet,	Harp
der dich erlöst durch seinen Tod,	Flute
den Himmel offenhaltet.	Violin
Fahr hin zu dem, der in der Tauf'	Violin
die Unschuld/dir gegeben,	Violin/Flute
er nehme dich/barmherzig/auf	Flute/Violin/Flute
in jenes/bess're/Leben.	Flute/Clarinet/Harp.

The double canon in the contrapuntal parts is scored in even more colourful fashion:

Leading part	Trp.	Fl.		Clar.	Trp.	Fl.	Trp.
Imitative part	Clar.	Trp.	Vl. Hp.		Clar.	Hp.	Clar.

Leading part	Fl.	Clar.		Trp.	Vl.	Clar.	Vl.
Imitative part	Hp.			Clar.	Hp.	Trp.	Trp.
						Hp.	
						Vl.	
						Hp.	

The interval-relationships in the two contrapuntal parts show how ready Webern was, to give prominence to the sounds themselves in spite of the strictness of formal construction: while the interval of imitation chosen for the two leading parts at the beginning remains the same throughout, though in the subsidiary double canon the interval is altered from bar 7 onwards (last crotchet in the trumpet part) and then kept.

Webern's use of sacred texts from Op. 12 No. 1 onwards is noteworthy. Stuckenschmidt sees this in relation to the events of the time, when he says: 'The worship of the Virgin and thoughts of the Passion exercised as much power on Webern in these war and post-war years as on many sculptors, painters and poets of expressionism. The Crucifixions and Pietàs of Ernst Barlach, Emil Nolde, Karl Schmidt-Rottluff, the sacred visions of Franz Werfel show a similar development.' In fact, Webern's creed was subjectively religious, and an actual place of worship is missing even in those works which are based on liturgical texts, as Stockhausen has pointed out.[1]

[1] *Melos*, 1957/250.

Five Canons on Latin Texts, Op. 16 for high soprano, clarinet and bass clarinet (1924)

  I   *Christus factus est pro nobis*
     (Philippians 2, 8–9)
  II *Dormi Jesu*
     (from *Des Knaben Wunderhorn*)
 III *Crux fidelis*
     (from the Good Friday liturgy)
 IV *Asperges me*
     (from the Maundy Thursday liturgy)
  V *Crucem tuam adoramus*
     (from the Good Friday liturgy)

What is a canon?—A piece of music in which several voices sing the same thing, only at different times. (Anton Webern, *Lectures*, p. 52.)

Since the chorus Op. 2 canonic writing is a key element in Webern's technique: it is the possibility of making identical material appear together with itself, by constantly varying displacement in time, in horizontal, vertical and 'diagonal' relationships, of creating an overall connection which would dissolve the different 'dimensions'—this can only become important in composition after the liquidation of thematicism, the concept of which never really allowed itself to be transformed into the vertical dimension. (Heinz-Klaus Metzger, *Reihe*, 2/43.)

If a composer writes canonically for voice and instruments, he is faced in principle with two possibilities (between which there are naturally many intermediate solutions). Firstly, he can write for the voice with the kind of intervals which has been regarded as typically vocal since the flowering of vocal polyphony, i.e. with a preference for small intervals. In this case he takes away from the accompanying instrument the possibility of real instrumental deployment. But if the composition is written from the point of view of the instrument, the voice too of necessity takes on an instrumental character. In Op. 15 No. 5 Webern adopted the first possibility: of the sixty-one intervals in the voice part no fewer than forty-six are unison, seconds and thirds. A look at the chronological table on p. 83 shows that this song was written as early as 1917, in the atmosphere of Opp. 13 and 14. But just in the following years Webern developed a highly expressive language of intervals in which the voice part takes on an apparently purely instrumental character, or rather it contains contrasts of intervals and pitch which, according to traditional ideas, are typically instrumental. The first four songs of Op. 15 (1921–2) are characteristic of this stage. In Op. 16 Webern adopted the second possibility: the external picture presented here is that of small canonic inventions which are more instrumental than vocal in character, in which the voice always enters after the instruments and never leads. The individual canons are as follows:

I   Three-part. Imitation at the major second between clarinet and soprano at a bar's distance: imitation between the two instruments at a half-bar's distance at the lower third in contrary motion. The instrumental parts are articulated by dynamics and typically instrumental means:

Ex. 63

In a middle section, *Propter quod*, with contrasting expression in which quaver movement predominates, the distance between the entries is cut by half.

Ex. 64

93

Note the minor second relationships in the writing of the individual parts as well as in the general ensemble. In the A section three-part minor second chords of the type noted before already appear, but in the middle section there is a strongly dissonant conglomeration in an extremely narrow space, a passage of a kind which Webern rarely wrote later. A much shortened recapitulation, *Quod est super*, is varied in that the entries appear at a crotchet's distance from the leading part in the canon.

II   Two-part. The voice imitates the clarinet in contrary motion.

Ex. 65

III   Three-part. Direct imitation. Intervals of a fourth and a tritone from the leading part at a distance of a crotchet.

Ex. 66

IV   Two-part. Imitation at the minor second (augmented octave) at a crotchet's distance.

94

Ex. 67
Op. 16, No. IV

V   Three-part. The voice imitates at the minor second and at
a crotchet's distance: the middle part begins another crotchet
later at a tritone from the leading part, in contrary motion.
Note the independent articulation of the two instrumental
parts.

Ex. 68
Op. 16, No. V

The Canons Op. 16 have been much discussed in writings on
Webern up to now, because through analysing them people tried
to reach significant conclusions regarding the 'constructive'
Webern. In this they tried, not without forcing the issue, to find
motivic relationships and formal divisions in connection with
these, which occasioned some minor polemics. One should not
forget that it has always been a characteristic of canonic writing
to lack not only periodic divisions but, particularly, motivic relationships in the individual part, as enough of these appear in the
imitations of it. Division into two or three sections would only
be necessary in a piece of greater length—see Bach's second Invention, for instance.

The assertion that Op. 16 is written in serial technique has been widely made, e.g. in Humphrey Searle's *Twentieth Century Counterpoint*, p. 79: 'The first canon of Webern's Op. 16 shows the use of a serial technique but is not based on a twelve-note series. As will be seen, this is a strict canon with one part an inversion, the voices entering at ever closer intervals towards the climax.' This is a typical mistake of the kind which often makes the literature on the Schoenberg school so problematic.[1] Schoenberg took over very many elements of traditional writing in his twelve-note Method. In an attempt to illustrate his roots in classical music, Beethoven's motivic working is mostly mentioned and the twelve-tone vocabulary is transferred to him unawares, so that he quickly becomes a 'predecessor' or 'prophet'. As an example Redlich says:[2] 'I have been able to find tendencies towards serial composition' and 'These experiments of Beethoven's are naturally not restricted to Op. 132. They are a particular characteristic of his late string quartets, which still await a morphological enquiry into their relationship with serial composition.' Beethoven no more composed 'pre-serially' than the Canons Op. 16 display serial technique. Their only relationship to serial technique is that the latter often uses canonic writing, which it took over from traditional techniques of composition.

THE ADOPTION OF SCHOENBERG'S 'METHOD OF COMPOSITION WITH TWELVE SEMITONES RELATED ONLY TO ONE ANOTHER'

Three Traditional Rhymes, Op. 17 (1924) for voice, violin (also viola), clarinet in B flat and bass clarinet in B flat

I   *Armer Sünder, du*
II *Liebste Jungfrau, wir sind dein*
III *Heiland, unsre Missetaten*

[1] *Mea culpa!* I should not have mentioned serial technique in connection with Op. 16 the canons of which are worked out on purely classical models, even if they have no tonality. (*Translator's note*).
[2] *Berg*, p. 27 f.

Three Songs, Op. 18 (1925), for voice, E flat clarinet and guitar

I   *Schatzerl klein, musst nit traurig sein*
II *Erlösung*, from *Des Knaben Wunderhorn*
    Mein Kind, sieh an die Brüste mein
III *Ave, Regina coelorum*

Two Songs, Op. 19 (1926) for mixed chorus with accompaniment of celesta, guitar, violin, clarinet and bass clarinet. Texts from Goethe's *Chinesische Jahres- und Tageszeiten.* Dedicated to Dr David Josef Bach[1]

I   *Weiss wie Lilien, reine Kerzen*
II *Ziehn die Schafe von der Wiese*

Otherwise, one composes as before—but on the basis of the series; one will have to invent on the basis of this fixed series. But rubbish can come out of it—as in tonal composition. The major and minor scales weren't responsible for that! (Webern 1932, *Lectures*, p. 53.)

As far as we can see most twelve-note composers have seen the reason for the existence and the purpose of the technique in the fact that it made it possible or at least easier to remain faithful to the basic stylistic idea of classical music, i.e. the development and variation of clearly defined musical ideas, in an idiom which is free of tonality. This way of thinking has allowed, even influenced the middle generation of twelve-note composers to neglect the inherent idea, of the twelve-note technique, i.e. the total determination of the musical continuity, and to stress the clearly existing characteristic of the twelve-note series as a melodic motif. Various technical procedures helped in this, such as the splitting up of the series into smaller groups, independent use of such groups, rotation of the notes within the groups, and so on. (Ernst Křenek, *Reihe*, 1955, 1/14.)

Twelve-note music is not a category. (Heinz-Klaus Metzger, *Reihe*, 1955 2/47.)

---

[1] Dr David Josef Bach, a friend of Schoenberg's youth and a Vienna city ocuncillor, in 1905 founded the Vienna Workers' Symphony Concerts, the direction of which he entrusted to Webern more and more from 1924 onwards. On 2 December 1933 in the Small Musikvereinssaal in Vienna he gave the address at a celebration in honour of Webern's 50th birthday which was arranged by the Austrian section of the International Society for Contemporary Music.

'The wearisome formal scruples of the composer of the old twelve-note style, which stubbornly insisted on the absurd necessity of expounding all four forms of his series mechanically one after the other, in the Utopian hope of winning the hearts of his audience and convincing them that in singing nowadays it is necessary to count up to twelve, are replaced by a concept of structure which is much stricter, but also much freer and less complicated.' (Niccolò Castiglioni, *Melos*, 1960, p. 372.)

In his lecture series *The Path to Composition with Twelve Notes* Webern gave a detailed account of the time in which Schoenberg, in a vast, far-reaching, constructive effort undertook the task of finding a principle for the construction of sound-material after the loss of tonal organization.

If we want to establish historically how this tonality suddenly disappeared and what started it, until Schoenberg finally saw one day quite intuitively how to restore order, then it was about 1908, when Schoenberg's Piano Pieces Op. 11 appeared. These were the first 'atonal' pieces: Schoenberg's first twelve-note work appeared in 1922. The interregnum was from 1908–1922: this stage lasted fourteen years, almost a decade and a half. But already in the spring of 1917—Schoenberg was living in the Gloriettegasse at that time and I was living near by—I called on him one fine morning to tell him that I had read in some newspaper where a few groceries could be hunted out. I disturbed him by my visit, and he explained to me that he was 'on the way to something quite new'. He didn't say more to me then, and I kept on worrying :'For God's sake, what can this be?'[1]

One day Schoenberg intuitively discovered the law which is the basis of twelve-note composition. By necessity it must follow from this law that one should give the sequence of the twelve notes a definite order. Today we have reached the end of this path, i.e. we have reached the goal: the twelve notes have come to power and the practical necessity of this law is perfectly clear to us nowadays. We can see its development without any gaps.[2]

[1] *Lectures*, p. 44.   [2] *Lectures*, p. 51.

Before discussing Webern's twelve-note works it is necessary to make the terminology clear. Schoenberg's method shows two principles:

1. Total chromaticism, called twelve-note writing in this book.
2. The use of series, called serial technique in this book.

Both these principles can appear separately: one can write twelve-note music without serial technique, and can also use serial technique on a diatonic basis. The combination of these two principles in the twelve-note method was a personal act of Schoenberg's own will, and Webern was convinced of its logical rightness and historical necessity. The fact that twelve-note writing and serial technique were not sufficiently kept separate either in the past, or nowadays, is a source of perpetual misunderstanding in the treatment of questions of modern music.

Opp. 17–19 show how Webern came to grips with the twelve-note method in the years 1924–6 and how systematically he explored its various possibilities, after first sceptically opposing Schoenberg's experiments. The twelve-note beginning of Op. 17 No. 1 could be based on the following series:

Ex. 69

In the second twelve-note group the order is already altered (8, 9, 7), and from the third total chromatic group, which overlaps with the second one, onwards it is only recognizable by occasional indications. Op. 17 No. 1 is not written with the twelve-note method (i.e. serially) but it is very much a twelve-note work. Eighteen twelve-note groups follow each other, in which occasionally some notes are missing and others appear twice.[1] What Webern used earlier, partly instinctively, partly consciously, and only in certain passages to create expressive tension and concentration, is used here systematically so as to become the constructive principle of a whole song:

[1] Perhaps the E sharp in the last bar is a printer's error?

Ex. 70
Op. 17, No. I, 1

(N.B. Clarinet and bass clarinet are written in B flat)

It is striking to find that the creation of harmonic 'strata' by ostinato figures or repetitions of notes, which had already played a part in the earlier works, is also carried over into Op. 17. It seems that the composer wished to set certain connecting forces against the total chromatic content. Motifs which appear in all the instrumental parts, such as the demisemiquaver motif in bar 7, also serve to unify the work. The voice part, in sharp contrast to the instruments throughout, is handled more or less as in Op. 15. The final bars show heightened expression, derived from the text:

Ex. 71   Op. 17, No. I, 14.

In Op. 17 No. 2 twenty-three twelve-note groups follow each other, but the basic order of the twelve chromatic notes is maintained exactly. It is remarkable with what mastery Webern handles material formed by a self-chosen rule:

Ex. 72

Op. 17, No, II, 13

(N.B. Clarinet and bass clarinet are written in B flat)

The following series is the basis of the song:

Ex. 73

Yet another technique is tried out in Op. 17 No. 3: the voice part goes through the basic series four and a half times.

Ex. 74

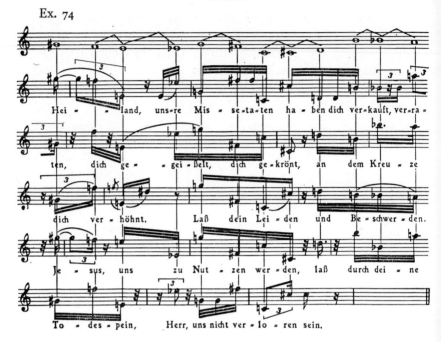

In the combination of the voice part with the instrumental parts this 'inverted passacaglia' is laid out in exactly the same way as the preceding pieces of this opus, i.e. in a chain of twelve-note groups. While the voice sings the series for the first time there are almost four groups of this kind, so that the series in the voice part only contributes a few notes now and then towards the building of the chromatic whole. The motifs in the instrumental parts are made up of the notes which are missing in the voice part:

Ex. 75

Op. 17, No. III, 1

(N.B. Clarinet and bass clarinet are written in B flat)

In principle this technique of combining very short motifs made out of segments of the series can be found in Webern's works ten years earlier, but in Op. 17 No. 3 it is used systematically. It is from this procedure that an important characteristic of Webern's lay-out of series can be explained—the predominance of minor seconds. Thus in the vertical dimension again and again we find chordal sounds of the kind that can be seen in Webern's works from Op. 3 onwards.

Leibowitz found that 'the handling of the twelve-note technique was still very rudimentary in Op. 17',[1] an opinion which has been widely reproduced elsewhere, e.g. by Rognoni: 'If the twelve-note technique in Op. 17 still appears indecisive. . . .'[2] Vlad on the other hand points out that there has been talk about Op. 17 'without anyone having had the opportunity of getting to know the whole work till 1955',[3] and establishes that, apart from the handling of the series, this music 'is much more refined and poised in expression than one would expect from Webern'.

The following Three Songs Op. 18 were only given a higher place in Webern's output by evolutionarily orthodox twelve-note theorists because in them the inversion of the series, the retrograde and the retrograde inversion also appear. But in the

[1] *Schoenberg*, p. 205.   [2] *Espressionismo*, p. 194.   [3] *Storia*, p. 54.

concentration and expressive tension which Webern's musical language had achieved, such differences of procedure are not audible. It may be important for the visual analyst whether total chromaticism is achieved through non-serially organized twelve-note groups as in Op. 17 No. 1, through twelve-note groups produced by serial technique as in Op. 17 No. 1, or by derivation from the basic series, but for the listener it is irrelevant. Attentive listening to the highly expressionistic group of works in Opp. 15–20 (1921–7) reveals no essential differences: at the most there can be heard an increasing concentration in which the systematic chromatic penetration of the writing certainly does play a part. Opinions on this point differ considerably: 'We saw in Op. 17 a big division in Webern's works.'[1] 'In these songs the step to the twelve-note system . . . is completed. With Schoenberg the step to the twelve-note system was taken after almost ten years of interior battle with himself and the material and had the effect of an explosion: with Webern the step happened almost unnoticeably, and his entry into the method hardly makes any appreciable difference in the works of his second period—there is certainly no break in style.'[2] '. . . The Trakl Songs, Op. 14, sound like twelve-note music. Webern then proved that the step to twelve-note music was a very small one and that it was not a principle coming in from the outside: his first twelve-note works, also songs with chamber ensemble, follow on without a break from the last works written in a free atonal style.'[3] And Eimert makes it clear: 'Webern's transition to twelve-note technique in Op. 17 does not mean a change in technique or even in style, but represents a completion of his technical apparatus.'[4]

The expressive tension, especially in the voice part, which almost goes beyond the bounds of possibility, gives Op. 18 such a very special flavour that one is not really tempted to try and make serial analyses of these pieces. In No. 2 the setting of Christ's words convinces one through the immediate expressiveness of the text:

[1] Stuckenschmidt, *Schöpfer*, p. 201.
[2] Zillig, *Variationen*, p. 187.
[3] Adorno, *Klangfiguren*, p. 172.   [4] *Reihe*, 2/39.

Ex. 76

Op. 18, No. II

It is strange that at this stage of his development Webern used this kind of treatment of the voice for quite different texts, e.g. also in No. 1 for the words *Schatzerl klein, musst nit traurig sein* (Little sweetheart, don't be sad). Whether one can call Webern a 'vocal composer par excellence'[1] on the strength of Op. 18 is a matter for thought. Fr. Herzfeld already said of the leaps of sevenths and ninths in Op. 5: 'These intervals do possess a high degree of tension. But the oftener they appear the more quickly they wear themselves out. A too harsh light makes one blind.'[2] Baldenius has studied the changes in the intervals in the vocal language from Op. 16 on and has argued with Eimert: 'The text finds no musical correspondence in this way, of the kind that could still be found in the George Songs. Here the words are "incorporated into the musical structure", as Eimert says (*Reihe*, 2/30). He goes so far as to say that the words are "hidden in an entirely new way" in this musical structure. I cannot fully subscribe to this positive evaluation: I have more of an impression that the text has been incorporated into the structure of the vocal line in a slightly ruthless way.'[3]

The same writer has shown us some interesting connections in the treatment of the series in Op. 18 No. 2:

The handling of the series and its other forms is here conditioned by the text. The three characters who speak in the poem,

---

[1] Jacques Wildberger.
[2] *Musica nova*, p. 86. [3] *Stiluntersuchungen*, p. 38.

the Virgin Mary, Christ and God the Father, each have their own form of the series: Mary has the basic series (BS), Christ in the dialogue with Mary the inversion of the series (I), in the dialogue with the Father a transposed retrograde inversion with the order of the notes somewhat freely arranged (RI 11), and the Father in the dialogue with Christ has the retrograde of the basic series (R). . . . This produces a structural division into four sections, but these are only made clear to the listener as changes of tempo. Each section ends with a ritardando and the next one begins *a tempo*. . . . I cannot say whether the choice of the different forms of the series for each person was caused by theological speculations.[1]

With the two choral songs Op. 19 Webern set himself a new problem which could be sketched thus, in a simplified manner: the work is written in a small number of parts, and the twelve chromatic notes are spread over a relatively long time-distance, unless very short note-values appear. But with the entry of each independent part this time-distance gets smaller, with far-reaching consequences for the tension of the music. (Schoenberg grappled with this problem in 1927–8 in the Variations for Orchestra Op. 31.) Occasional doubling would have destroyed the balance of the twelve chromatic notes and can produce tonal points of emphasis, but regular doubling thickens up the texture. Webern arranges his five-part instrumental ensemble in such a way that two harmony instruments (celesta and guitar) chiefly take part in the serial construction, while the melody instruments are built into the choral part. This has led to the assertion that it was done 'to facilitate the intonation of the chorus'.[2] A glance at the score corrects this assertion:

[1] Op. cit. p. 45f.　　　[2] Leibowitz, *Schoenberg*, p. 206.

Ex. 77

Op. 19, No. I, 9

If a choir has not managed to pitch the notes on its own, the strings coming in later (in pp) will not be of much help. Webern was clearly more interested in giving the strings rhythmical motifs as additional structural elements than in writing additional supporting parts. Even in passages where the intention of supporting the chorus is quite clear, e.g. in the fugato from bar 17 on of the same piece, the rhythmical-constructive intention probably predominates.

String Trio, Op. 20 (1927)

Webern's new conception, completely developed, appears for the first time in the String Trio: so it is the first of his works which cannot be followed harmonically and melodically in the traditional way. (Heinz-Klaus Metzger, 'Webern and Schoenberg', *Reihe* 2/49.)

The String Trio was published in the same year in which it was composed, by Universal Edition. Erwin Stein, Webern's friend from Schoenberg's composition class, wrote an introduction to it which was clearly authorized by the composer. This says:

... the principle of developing a movement by the variation of motifs and themes is the same as in the classical masters. However in his manner of developing the motifs and in his thematic treatment Webern deviates a great deal from the classical examples. Motifs and themes are varied more radically here, and whenever they recur it is in a very modified form. One note-series provides the basic material for the whole piece, as in Schoenberg's 'Composition with twelve notes related only to one another'. The parts are composed in a mosaic-like manner from segments of the series. Through various combinations these create continually changing sounds. There is a close analogy with the kaleidoscope, which continuously produces new effects by varied groupings of a number of colours and elements of form.

The two-movement work—an introduction to the second movement, *Sehr getragen und ausdrucksvoll*, replaces the classical middle movement—consists of a Rondo and a sonata movement: with its length of nine and a half minutes[1] it marks an important point in Webern's development; according to Zillig 'the decisive turning-point'.[2] 'The return to the large form'[3] after the instrumental miniatures and a series of eight vocal *opera*, contradicts the legend of Webern's 'straight line' type of development, unless one wishes to see the straight line in the inner necessity for so radical a change. And yet the generally held view is that it was Schoenberg's twelve-note method which first made large forms possible again. Webern himself believed this: 'Only after Schoenberg pronounced the law, did larger forms become possible again.'[4] And Leibowitz says: 'the large form, made possible by the twelve-note technique'.[5] Křenek[6] is of the same opinion: 'In the pre-dodecaphonic period of the so-called "free" atonality there was not much attempt at the development and execution of larger forms. Historically this has been the endeavour of the middle generation of twelve-note composers.' But he adds the following qualifica-

[1] This is the timing given in the score: the performance in the complete recording takes 8 min. 16 sec. (*Translator's note*).
[2] *Variationen*, p. 187.   [3] Leibowitz, *Schoenberg*, p. 206.
[4] *Lectures*, p. 54.   [5] *Schoenberg*, p. 206.   [6] *Reihe*, 1/15.

tion: 'One can in fact follow the classical ideal of development and variation of ideas even in the atonal idiom without subjecting the latter to the twelve-note discipline, but it must be said that endeavours only led to valid results after the strict twelve-note technique had been mastered.'

A look at the composer's workshop shows how far this view is true. The first movement is built in a classical rondo form with the following scheme (this exposition of it differs a little from that in the foreword to the score):

Introduction	Bars	1– 3
A		4–10
B		10–15
A	`	16–21
C		22–30 (repeated in bars 31–40)
Introduction		41–43
A		44–51
B		51–56
A		57–62
Coda		62–65

The series from which the whole work is developed is rich in semitonal relations:

Ex. 78

Thus there is a complex system of minor second intervals, in both the horizontal and vertical dimensions; these are especially prominent in the large number of two-note motifs. The series in its basic form and its retrograde make up the introduction as a kind of exposition, in which notes 11 and 12, in long note-values, act as the bridge to the retrograde form. The whole work consists of a concentrated sequence of twelve-note groups woven out of the various forms of the series and their transpositions. Webern solves the problem of building larger formal units from these twelve-note groups by developing a seven-bar theme (A) from bar 4 onwards which according to the rondo design appears four times in the movement. This twenty-seven-note theme is in no way twelve-note in itself; for instance the note C occurs four times, in three of these in long note-values in exposed positions:

Ex. 79   Op. 20, No. 1, 4

(theme in viola)

As in section A, section C is dominated by a nine-bar theme which is developed in the same way. It is as little twelve-note as the theme of the A section, and it stretches through seven twelve-note groups which are in the order RI 6, R 1, I 8, RI 10, R 2, R 4 and BS 4 (BS = Basic Series; I = Inversion of the series; R = Retrograde; RI = Retrograde Inversion: the numbers give the interval of transposition—see p. 38.) It would also have been possible for Webern to build long thematic and therefore formal lines on a twelve-note, or nearly twelve-note basis from the compositional position of the cello pieces Op. 11. The reason why Webern did not develop these at the time was probably less due to the lack of a technical aid to composition than to his manner of expressing himself in 1914, which had found the short form adequate for his needs. What now led him to write in larger forms again was not conditioned by his mastery of the material offered by the twelve-note method, but by an inner clarification which becomes even more apparent in Op. 21 and is the real characteristic of Webern's later style. Adorno states, aptly, on this question: 'The assertion, which has often been repeated since Erwin Stein's programme note of 1924, that in the style of free atonality no large instrumental forms were possible, has not been proved.'[1]

The construction of the themes in Op. 20 has also been discussed in writings on Webern, e.g. by Zillig: 'Anton Webern had become somewhat separated from Schoenberg, especially with the String Trio Op. 20 of 1927. . . . All his works up to his tragic death were certainly strict twelve-note compositions, but they entirely avoid the technique of classical theme construction and working-out which Schoenberg had rediscovered.'[2]

In connection with the larger form Webern was once again faced with the problem of the repetition or return of larger and smaller formal sections. Even the simplest, classical method— repeat marks—is found in the second movement of the String Trio (bars 10–73a). Webern probably realized quite clearly that the danger of any loss of tension through the recognition of a formal group which had already been heard and fully grasped was very slight here. Webern's attitude to the problem of repetition, which had changed fundamentally since his early works, particularly after Opp. 5–11, was unequivocally expressed in a lecture given a few years after the composition of Op. 20: 'How can I achieve comprehensibility in the easiest way? By repetition. All formal construction is built up on this, all musical forms are based on this principle.'[3]

Apart from the repeat in the second movement, all the repeated material is considerably transformed. As an example, here is the C theme of the first movement in its original form and its varied return:

Ex. 80

[1] *Philosophie*, p. 63.   [2] *Musica*, 60/78.   [3] *Lectures*, p. 22.

Apart from the first bar it would hardly be possible for anyone to grasp its identity by ear alone. And in the A section, which comes four times, comprehension becomes almost impossible because of a similar technique of variation, through the change in octave pitch of individual notes, and by the continual crossing of widely spaced melodic lines. 'The individual parts can no longer be followed in this method of treating the material, for, through the frequent leaps and crossings of the parts, through the continual, if purposive, changes in the expression and tone colour of each single note, the principle of polyphony, valid up till now, seems to have been abolished. The parts written in the score are only an external means of realizing the work in practice, just as the barlines only serve to make ensemble playing possible.'[1] Stravinsky alluded to these aural experiences when he wittily defended himself against the reproach of using classical forms, which the militant followers of Webern kept bringing against him: 'The Schoenberg, Berg and Webern of the 1920s were regarded in those days as the most extreme iconoclasts, but today it appears that they used musical form in the same way as myself: "historically". I used it openly: they carefully concealed it. Take for example the Rondo of Webern's Trio: the music is marvellously interesting, but no one could recognize it as a Rondo.'[2]

The String Trio Op. 20 gave Webern dismal experiences with the public and performers; for instance in the eyes of the critic Alfred Heuss, who was enormously influential at that time, it made him appear as the symbol of musical decadence. The work was hissed at a Festival of the ISCM—at that time not yet a 'world music festival'—in Siena in 1928, and also caused dissension at other performances. Hans Kuznitzky[3] wrote of a performance at the composers' festival in Schwerin: 'Webern's Trio was regarded as "atonal" and the diligent hissing of the festival audience showed that they failed to understand it. Though one must admit that without a score it would be difficult to grasp the contrapuntal filigree-work of this creation which scurries by like a shadow, this does not say anything against the work in question. Whether this

[1] Zillig, *Variationen*, p. 189.   [2] *Melos*, 1958/57.   [3] *Neue Musikzeitung*, 1928/688.

is a path that can be followed is doubtful: but the inviolability of the composer's will cannot be invalidated by hisses.' In a letter to Emil Hertzka, the Director of the Universal Edition, Webern wrote on 19 September 1928: 'Kolisch's[1] report on a demonstration regarding my Trio—he cabled me: "First disturbance, then uproar, finally triumph!"—made me extremely agitated on your behalf. Now your kind card has again convinced me of your unshakable belief in my cause.' But on 29 April 1938 Webern wrote to Willi Reich: 'Did you hear about the ghastly incident at the performance of my String Trio in London? The cellist got up, saying: "I can't play this thing!" and *walked off the platform*! Surely nothing like that has ever happened before!' [2]

Symphony, Op. 21 (1928) for clarinet, bass clarinet, two horns,
      harp, 1st and 2nd violins, viola and cello

To my daughter Christine

By 'art' I mean the capacity of presenting an idea in the clearest, simplest, that means 'most comprehensible' form. . . . And therefore I have never understood what 'classical', 'romantic' and so on are; nor have I put myself in opposition to the masters of the past, but have always tried to match them —to present as clearly as possible what it has been entrusted to me to say. (To Hildegarde Jone, 6 August 1928, shortly after finishing the symphony.)

If one listens to Opp. 15–20 one immediately after the other, unprejudiced by analytical results, from the mode of expression one gets the impression that the adoption of the twelve-note method as well as the return to larger forms took place in a group of works which are very much linked together in style. But a random glance at any page of the scores of Opp. 20 and 21—which can be confirmed at once even by a superficial listening to the music— shows that in the symphony something essentially new in Webern's development has taken place: the score is full of rests, and not only at the beginning, to present an economical, restrained exposition (see Ex. 82, p. 116), but throughout. Matching this,

---

[1] Kolisch was a well-known violinist, leader of the Kolisch Quartet and a pioneer in the performance of Schoenberg's works.
[2] *Lectures*, p. 58.

the motivic development, which in Op. 20 was largely concealed from the listener and reserved for readers of the score, here becomes audible again, at least in the essential intervals. Such a fundamental change could be regarded as a conscious attempt to bring the listener back again, suggested by considerations of communication based on Webern's experiences in his last preceding works. He once mentioned sociological questions in one of the lectures: 'Naturally it is nonsensical to advance "social" objections: Why don't people understand that? . . . How do people hope to follow like that? Obviously it is very difficult.'[1]

One may come closer to the secret impulse behind this change by regarding the renewed approach to the listener in Op. 21 as the fading away of the kind of expression which demanded an eruptive outlet, and through which, in a period of the strongest expressionism, the 'I' had become so much the central point of artistic assertions that all stylistic details were controlled from this centre. But the change in Webern can be seen in conjunction with the general development in Europe:

It is very revealing to notice how, after the relative narrowness and similarity of all compositions of the radical expressionistic phase about 1918, creations which differed essentially from each other began to appear, step by step, in the 'clarified' expressionistic phase round about 1928. The unity of the entire development of modern music from 1911 to 1934 can be rightly called 'Expressionism' if we differentiate between the violent years of outbreak with their many excesses—the 'radical' phase—and the second, 'purified', period, in which, without any sacrifice of the basic ideas and standpoint, the more orderly, measured and cooler spirit and balance of forces won the upper hand.[2]

If developments round about 1928 often led to neo-classicism of many different kinds, this only shows that it worked differently in each composer. One could have called many things in Webern 'neo-classical', for instance the return to classical types of form, if the word had not become an aesthetic term of abuse aimed at Stravinsky in particular.

[1] *Lectures*, p. 45.　　　[2] Siegfried Borris, *Über Wesen*, p. 51 f.

The Symphony Op. 21 is in two movements. The first movement, as can be observed by both eye and ear, is divided into two
sections, of twenty-four and forty bars respectively, which are
both repeated, while the second contains the markings Theme,
seven Variations and Coda. All this expresses an aesthetic position
which is in radical contrast to nearly all Webern's previous works.
The symphony, like all Webern's works from Op. 20 on, is based
on a single series, semitones predominating in its structure.

Ex. 81

But this series also shows a further relationship which is characteristic of Webern's serial thinking: it is built as a palindrome, i.e. it
consists of the same intervals reading from both ends towards the
middle. As a result the basic series is identical with the transposed
retrograde, and so are the inversions of both. This excludes half
the possibilities of different forms of the series, but the series
provides a large number of motivic relationships within itself.
The work is so arranged as a cycle that in the Theme of the second
movement a form of the series (RI 2 = I 8) appears in its most
'comprehensible' shape and is then the subject of variations;
the first movement acts as a kind of prelude to the variations.
An exact analysis of it by Leibowitz has introduced us to the marvellous structure of the first movement: one can readily concur
with his remark: 'It is only after patient analysis that one discovers,
for example, the double canon in contrary motion in four parts
with which the symphony begins.'[1] This four-part canon is
divided between nine instruments in a way which was largely
anticipated in the song Op. 15 No. 5.

[1] *Schoenberg*, p. 211.

Ex. 82

Op. 21, No. I

* * Klingen wie notiert

In an analytical study[1] Siegfried Borris has shown that the beginning of the symphony is based on a 'rotational' chord, a chord of five fourths and its mirror form, round the axis of A, the first note of the series:

Ex. 83

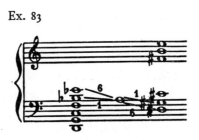

Similar mirror-chords are often found in Webern's late works, and György Ligeti has made a comprehensive study of those in the First Cantata.[2]

The compositional procedures in the Symphony reveal much about the change in Webern's musical thinking. In the canon of the first movement and also in the first variation four forms of the series appear simultaneously. In such a manner of composition it is impossible, apart from actual repetitions, to avoid the return of the same notes in a small number of bars. All the twelve notes of the scale do not appear till the 23rd note is reached; twelve-note orthodoxy would maintain that there are eleven 'wrong' notes. A basic rule of Schoenberg's which Webern followed in his Opp. 17–20 is disregarded here: Webern clearly knew that for the negative part of the twelve-note method, the avoidance of tonal relationships, an approximation to total chromaticism is quite sufficient. On the other hand serial technique has come into the foreground of interest, as giving the possibility of the most concentrated polyphonic writing. For Webern the series was the basic cell, an idea which he often expressed: 'Goethe's primeval plant: the root is no different from the stalk, the stalk no different from the leaf, the leaf again no different from the flower: variations of the same idea.'[3] 'The same law applies to all living things:

[1] 'Synopsis', in *Stilporträts*. [2] *Über die Harmonik* . . .
[3] *Lectures*, p. 53.

"variations on a Theme".—That is the primeval form which is at the root of everything. Something which apparently is quite different is really the same. The most comprehensive unity results from this.'[1] 'So this is the "primeval plant" we discussed recently!— Always different and yet always the same! Wherever we cut into the piece we can always find the course of the series. This ensures unity.'[2]

Webern himself analysed the second movement of the Symphony in a lecture: 'The series is. . . . It has the peculiarity that the second half is the retrograde of the first half. This is a very intimate unity. So here only 24 forms are possible, as two are always identical with each other. At the beginning the retrograde appears in the accompaniment of the theme, the first variation is, in the melody, a transposition of the series starting on C. The accompaniment is a double canon.—Greater unity cannot be achieved. Even the Netherlanders never managed this.—In the fourth variation there are constant mirror forms. This variation itself is the central point of the whole movement, and after this everything goes backwards. So the whole movement itself is a double canon by retrograde motion. . . . What you see here— retrograde, canon etc.,—it's always the same—mustn't be thought of as "stunts"—that would be absurd!—As many connections as possible were to be created, and you must admit that there are many connections here!'[3]

Here is the theme:

Ex. 84

[1] *Lectures*, p. 53.　　[2] *Lectures*, p. 55.　　[3] *Lectures*, p. 60.

118

The fifth variation shows how different strata of sound are built with the changed serial technique.

Ex. 85

Notes 1–4 and 9–12 of the series are compressed into chords and between them comes a symmetrically built harp motif 7–8–5–6–5–8–7, which is heard five times. 'But the sound of the harp, which adds its complementary four notes, always in a different order, to the persistent eight notes of the strings, is changed here into the ancient sound of herd bells, the last ultimate soul-moving sound in the mountains,' Adorno says of this passage.[1] It has already been stressed in the discussion of Webern's earlier works that 'strata-construction' of this kind is diametrically opposed to the principle of dodecaphony. But here we can see clearly what a change has taken place in Webern's sensitivity to sound in respect of material which still remains unaltered, i.e. minor second chords: in the early works the chord is the primary element out of which the melody develops, but in Op. 21 the linear conception is in the foreground, and the chord arises from the addition of notes of the series together. In his works Webern had already reached twelve-tonality, arising out of expressive tension, at a time when Schoenberg had hardly dreamed of the twelve-note method. In the latter—or rather in that part of the method which is concerned with twelve-tonality or dodecaphony, the expressionist means of expression was petrified. Webern rejected this part of the 'law' in its rigid form at the very moment when he changed his manner of expression to a 'clarified expressionism'.

[1] A.W., *Lecture*, 21 April 1932.

Quartet, Op. 22 (1930) for violin, clarinet, tenor saxophone and piano

To Adolf Loos[1] on his 60th birthday

I   *Sehr mässig*
II *Sehr schwungvoll*

Yes, this Quartet is a miracle. What staggered me above everything else was its originality. (Alban Berg to Webern, 19 August 1932.)

In this work too Webern occupied himself above all with the problem of using the series in several strata with the use of mirror effects. By the use of basic or retrograde series and inversions at a short time distance, the writing gives the impression of a canon in contrary motion. But the distance of the imitation entries varies, and fluctuates in time values between 3/8 and 1/16. The theme (bars 6–15, which are repeated) appears in the tenor saxophone like a cantus firmus[2] and is developed from BS and BS 6. This melodic kernel, presented by one instrument only, is surrounded by two other parts, in which at first I 6 and BS 7, and from bar 12 I and BS 10 in semiquavers are used. In contrast to the theme these are split up in sound, being divided between piano and violin or clarinet. From this use of intervals arises a thick net of motivic relations like in a chorale prelude where subsidiary parts are built out of the canto fermo. In the five introductory bars I and BS 10 are coupled together—the two-part writing and variable distance of the entries show that these bars are of a preparatory nature. Still looser in the texture of the parts is the second movement, of which Webern said to Willi Reich that formally it was constructed in a very similar way to the Scherzo from Beethoven's Sonata Op. 14 No. 2.[3]

In Op. 22 the struggle between the two principles of polyphonic

Ex. 86

Op. 22, No. I, 21

---

[1] 1870–1933, a prominent architect who was a friend of Schoenberg, Berg and Webern and a strong supporter of their cause.

[2] Leibowitz.   [3] *Lectures,* p. 63.

writing and avoidance of a central tonality through twelve-note groups can again be seen. In passages like Ex. 86 four series cross in two strata and produce four F sharps as close together as possible, which Webern would certainly have avoided in his early twelve-note works.

There is a striking division of the line into motifs of two, three or at the most four notes in short values, divided by rests as well. Although this can be found earlier in Webern's works, in Op. 22 it is brought to a higher pitch than ever before. It gives the work a very loose, almost playful character, which is increased by the thinness of the writing; it also makes for a certain uniformity, as there are too few contrasts and the possibilities of counteracting this with concentration of the writing are also too few. This 'pointillist style', in which the texture is woven out of small melodic particles, has exerted an extraordinary influence in the years since 1950. An event described by Peter Stadlen throws some light on the interpretation of works of this kind: 'I think it was in Vienna early in 1937 that I accompanied Webern to a concert where his symphony was being performed. Webern felt rather gloomy, because the conductor (who is still world-famous today) has not spent nearly enough time discussing the work with him— and there had been occasional waves of mirth during rehearsals. The moment the performance was over, Webern turned to me and said with some bitterness: "A high note, a low note, a note in the middle—like the music of a madman!" '[1] So Webern did not aim at 'atomizing' the melody, but at the unity which comes from the dovetailing of small melodic segments into each other.

A review by Heinrich Kralik of a performance of the Symphony Op. 21 shows the way this style was regarded round about 1930: 'Webern's music is realized more or less in that sphere where the last, most refined threads of impressionism come to their end, where only the fibres flutter in the air, in the atmospheric plane, in the whirlwind dance of sounding sundust.'[2] But even in 1957 Dallin puts the only Webern example in his book under 'Fragmentation', points out the 'pointillism' and says: 'Few would be tempted to follow in Webern's footsteps all the way, so perhaps

[1] *Score*, 22/12.   [2] *Die Musik*, 1930/542.

it is superfluous to warn that to do so probably would prove to be artistically fatal.'[1]

Three Songs, Op. 23 (1933–4) from *Viae Inviae* of Hildegard Jone for voice and piano

To the Poet

I   *Das dunkle Herz, das in sich lauscht*
II   *Es stürzt aus Höhen Frische, die uns leben macht*
III *Herr Jesus mein, Du trittst mit jedem Morgen ins Haus*

Three Songs, Op. 25 (1934–5) on poems of Hildegard Jone for voice and piano

I   *Wie bin ich froh*
II   *Des Herzens Purpurvogel fliegt durch Nacht*
III *Sterne, Ihr silbernen Bienen der Nacht*

I am very glad that these songs—there are six of them, three each from Op. 23 and 25—will have their first performance at the evening planned by you in Basle—they are already almost ten years old. (To Willi Reich, 23 October 1943.)

Between the Quartet Op. 22 of 1930 and the Songs Op. 23 there is a creative gap of almost three years. Webern, who worked slowly and under the most difficult material conditions, often needed creative pauses of this kind; between Opp. 8 and 9 he did not finish a work for two years, and there was another 'silent period' after the Piano Variations Op. 27. In the years after 1930 it was pretty certainly unfavourable external circumstances which strongly oppressed the extremely sensitive composer. Brief passages from his letters hint at more than they say: '. . . in the last few weeks I have had such horrible things to do professionally as perhaps never before!'[2] '. . . besides that many lessons, the course you know about, etc. So I can't get down to composing.'[3] 'Here in Vienna it is getting more and more dreadful—what they

---

[1] *Technique*, p. 198.
[2] To Hildegard Jone, 27 September 1930.
[3] To Humplik and Jone, 11 February 1932.

are inflicting on me almost every day is hardly bearable any more. . . . Perhaps the salvation from these horrible Viennese conditions will come for me. I want to work, dearest friends!'[1] 'I am in terrible trouble: I am more and more oppressed by having no time for composition. Quite spontaneously one day I began the composition of your beautiful, wonderful poem; but I had to interrupt it soon, and now I am being revenged for allowing myself only to sit down to my own work now and then in January and February. Now I am so behindhand with the other things, the preparations for my concerts, here and in London. How shall I get through it all?'[2] 'Now I am working again at last . . . I feel that I have never felt the condition of working as sensitively as now. I hope it will last a little!'[3]

For professional reasons Webern had moved from Mödling to Vienna, but could not stand it there ('Up till now I have been completely out of balance.'[4] '. . . we cannot get used to the new state of things'[5]) and he went back to Mödling. In these years his work as a conductor increased a good deal in amount. In addition to his regular Viennese performances, in which among other works he conducted Mahler symphonies, the *Kindertotenlieder*, the *Actus Tragicus* and the Brahms Requiem, he also had concerts in Barcelona and London ('. . . in 6 days I had 33 hours of orchestral rehearsals and had to give two concerts'[6]).

Apart from external reasons which hindered composition, inner ones must have been at work as well. After seven years Webern again turned to setting texts, an occupation which had engaged him exclusively for a long time in his middle period. Now he found an adequate medium of expression in the piano, which he had not used in vocal composition since about 1916, probably because it did not correspond to his expressive style of that time. Webern, who painted in restrainedly glowing colours during his highly expressionist period, whose pressing aim for a long time was the discovery of new sound-colours, has now become principally a draughtsman. The use of serial technique in strata in Opp. 21 and

---

[1] To Humplik, 8 March 1932.   [2] To Hildegard Jone, 3 March 1933.
[3] To Hildegard Jone, 6 January 1934.   [4] 12 January 1932.
[5] 11 February 1932.   [6] To Humplik and Jone, 3 May 1933.

22 confirms this. But his attitude to the vocal line has also changed. In the middle group of works it was overstrained with a rich variety of extreme notes up to the furthest limits of expression, handled in a similar way to the instruments and forming part of the general writing in this way. But now the vocal writing has become calmer, especially in places where clarified tranquillity emanates from the text. A passage like

Ex. 87   Op. 23, No. 1, 45

could almost be found in Reger's *Schlichte Weisen*. But the expressionistic treatment of the voice in wide intervals is found, for instance, in the second song, and here is demanded by the text. Webern's language has achieved constrasts, which are an essential characteristic of the later cantatas. A really vocal handling of the voice part in long lines, in which the rests which stem from the declamation have a connecting rather than a dividing function, are striking in the whole of Op. 23. But Ex. 87 also shows another sign of stylistic change: the F in bar 47 is involuntarily heard as a leading note, E sharp, to the F sharps two notes before and after it. Such relationships can be found in the series itself, the layout of which differs very considerably from Webern's practice in Opp. 17–22:

Ex. 88

It contains only one minor second, and the structure is dominated by seven thirds. This results in the formation of tonal groups (the diminished triad E flat, G flat, C: the augmented triad C–E–G sharp, the F major sequence F–A–B flat). Such a layout of the series could have been due to suggestions by Berg, whose handling of the twelve-note method strongly aimed at the retention of tonal relations (the series on which his violin concerto is based could stand as an example of what not to do in any primer of the twelve-note method). Through this kind of construction of note-groups,

and the fact that the voice and piano are no longer in a complementary harmonic relationship, astonishingly traditional sound-
formations appear, as for instance Op. 23 No. 1 bar 34 with the
augmented triad C–E–G sharp and a clear feeling of A minor.
Because of the almost complete removal of the minor second as
a basic interval for the construction of sounds, the many major
sevenths and diminished ninths disappear from the part-writing;
they had been necessary in the past for the avoidance of 'Tristan-
esque' chromatic tension. The songs of Op. 23 are once again
'easier' to sing. Singers who want to perform Webern are
recommended to try Opp. 3, 4, 8 and 12, and then to get on to
the late songs before tackling those of the middle period.

In contrast to the Symphony Op. 21 and the Quartet Op. 22,
serial technique is here used for the voice-and-piano relationship.
Although the whole of Op. 23 is developed from one series, the
voice part is created from forms of the series which are independent
of the 'accompaniment'. But the piano part contains twelve-note
groups, sometimes in a narrow space, whose chordal structure
often hardly uses the polyphonic possibilities of the series. In
some ways this layout seems to look back to Op. 17 No. 3, but it
stems here from the desire to achieve a contrasting and individual
treatment of voice and piano. This contrast in itself gives Op. 23
a peculiar charm, and one can understand Leibowitz speaking of
a 'breath of Schubert'[1] and a 'wholly singing character, I would
call it almost Schubertian'.[2] This contrast can be clearly seen in
the first bars of Op. 23 No. 1:

Ex. 89

Op. 23, No. I.

[1] *Schoenberg*, p. 211.   [2] *Introduction*, p. 239.

In Op. 25 No. 1 we find a similar dexterity in inventing easily comprehensible motivic shapes out of the twelve-note groups in the piano part and using them throughout the song:

Ex. 90

Op. 25, No. I (Beginning)

It is remarkable that in the whole of the first set of songs (Op. 23) Webern used only the four basic forms of the series and their transposition at the tritone. In Op. 25 the choice of the forty-eight possibilities of serial formation is even more characteristic:

I   BS, I 2, R, RI
II   BS 5, I 7, R 5, RI 5
III   as I, with one exception.

This is an attempt to create contrasts from the nature of the sound-material, rather as Debussy sometimes introduces pentatonic writing and whole-tone scales into different formal sections and Bartók, in the same spirit, uses different possibilities of scale-formation.

Op. 23 is the first of a group of five vocal works, Opp. 23, 25, 26, 29 and 31, in which Webern set texts of the Viennese painter and poet Hildegard Jone exclusively.[1] Together with her husband, the sculptor Josef Humplik, she was a friend of Webern's from 1926 to his death, and by her understanding interest in Webern's work, she must have meant a great deal to him as a person as well as in creative stimulus in his increasing outer and inner loneliness. As early as 1934, in a little essay dedicated to Webern, she found words which express everything essential about him: 'If the life

[1] For the sources of the texts see Anton Webern, *Briefe an H. Jone und J. Humplik*, p. 69.

of an artist like Anton Webern lacks everything superfluous, all desire for the world or for company, all spiritual decoration, we must clearly understand that his art gives us the marvel of the greatest conceivable terseness in the essential and the real. Only where life and art are confined to the most important things can their wealth of these be unfolded. Every small part of such an activity—in which everything is ordered, like the dust on a butterfly's wings—somehow shows the whole of his spiritual nature.'[1]

In this volume of letters, which is of fundamental importance for the understanding of the man as well as the artist, this couple have created a literary memorial of lasting value to Webern—and themselves. The text of Op. 23 No. 1 is an example of Hildegard Jone's world of thought and feeling and its verbal expression:

The dark heart, which hearkens to itself,
sees spring not only by the breeze and scent
which blossom through its glow:
it feels spring in the dark realm of roots,
which reaches to the dead:
That which grows lays its tender roots
on that which waits in the dark:
it drinks strength and repose from the night
before it gives itself to the day,
before as a chalice of love it sends its fragrance to heaven
and before a golden flutter from heaven bears it life.
I do not belong to myself.
The springs of my soul,
they flow into the meadows of him who loves me,
and make his flowers blossom and are his.
You do not belong to yourself.
The rivers of your soul,
O man beloved by me,
they flow into mine

[1] From 23, a Viennese musical journal, 1934, Vol. 14, dedicated to Anton Webern on his 50th birthday. Reprinted in *Briefe an H. Jone und J. Humplik*, p. 70.

so that it will not wither.
We do not belong to ourselves,
not you, not I, not anyone.

The exchange of letters give an exhaustive account of the creation of Op. 23 and Webern's formal plans in general. The first decision was made as early as 1930: 'Now I would like to ask you a great favour: since I have known your literary work I cannot get rid of the idea of setting some of it to music. That is why at one time I suggested that you should write opera texts, or rather dramatic texts, and now I have the following idea. I must say first that your very fine dramatic poems did not find me in the right readiness for such work, although at that time I had the idea very seriously of writing something of this kind. You know only too well yourself what can happen in this respect and I am perhaps a specially extreme case. It almost always comes out differently from what I *apparently* wanted. Now I am very occupied with the idea of writing a cantata. And my request is: would you be willing to write a text of this kind for me?'[1] In the letter of 3 March 1933 quoted earlier Webern describes the beginning of his work on the text. A few months later the third part is finished: 'I have worked well. One of your texts, which fulfil my hopes more and more, is already set. That is from *Herr Jesus mein* to *Und, ewig Schlafende, auch euch erwartet Tag.* And now I am making *Es stürzt aus Höhen Frische*—how wonderful these words are—down to *überglüht noch lange Glut* into a second song. But the sequence of the two songs will correspond to that of your poems. How deeply they move me! And I am happy at last to be in this position—of setting your words. I have wanted it for a long time.'[2] 'For the present I have finished the setting of texts from your *Viae Inviae.* It has come out as I intended: 1st song, *Es stürzt aus Höhen* to *den Himmel und die Seele überglüht noch lange Glut.* 2nd song: *Herr Jesus mein* to *auch Euch erwartet Tag.* . . . I say "for the present", as I have the feeling that I shall soon have to come back to words of yours. However I think these two songs should remain by themselves for the moment at any rate. Together they make a musical whole:

[1] To H. Jone, 8 September 1930.   [2] To H. Jone, 27 July 1933.

in the sense of a certain contrast between them.'[1] 'Now at last I am at work again. It is *Das dunkle Herz, das in sich lauscht.* Everything which comes after that up to where I was before: *Es stürzt aus Höhen Frische,* will come before this song and the following one, *Herr Jesus mein,* as in your order.'[2] 'Meanwhile the third song is finished. As it contains the words from *Das dunkle Herz* to *ich und du und alle* it has become quite long and in musical form is a kind of "Aria", consisting of a slow section and from *Ich bin nicht mein* a quicker one, but which has the tempo marking *ganz ruhig* [very calm]. This second part is almost kept down to a whisper. Perhaps you can more or less see from this description how I have interpreted the second section of your words in particular: after a great outburst in the first section complete silence, calm, simplicity.'[3]

It is clear that Webern thought of the three Songs Op. 25, which were partly written during the composition of the Concerto Op. 24, as a unified cycle: this emerges both from interrelations in the text and from the fact that they are all based on the same series. The structure of the latter is characteristic of what Webern now means by a series, i.e. a means of obtaining unity through intervallic structure. The series of Op. 21 was a palindrome in intervals: in the series of Op. 25 one motif comes three times:

Ex. 91

This produces a strong unification of the motivic elements. The series is very freely treated in the work: missing notes in the voice part are supplied by the piano, and vice versa; a form of the series is begun by one performer and continued by the other; the motif which comes three times in the series produces a partial identity of pitch with transpositions of itself and makes it possible to have two sections of the series in one part with notes missed out. One gets the impression of an almost ironical superiority to the Method, but also that of a virtuosity in serial technique which reaches heights of artistic ingenuity and seems to regard the technique as

---

[1] To H. Jone, 3 September 1933. [2] To H. Jone, 6 January 1934.
[3] To H. Jone, 20 March 1934.

an end in itself. But this in itself frees the composer from being too restricted by rules and gives him a new creative freedom.

Concerto, Op. 24 (1934) for flute, oboe, clarinet, horn, trumpet, trombone, violin, viola and piano

To Arnold Schoenberg on his 60th birthday

I *Etwas lebhaft*
II *Sehr langsam*
III *Sehr rasch*

It is obvious that everything which has been and will be said about Webern's technique and style of composition will not demonstrate that he wrote beautiful music. Many musicians have not escaped from the mistaken idea that the Concerto Op. 24, for instance, or the Piano Variations, or any other work in which one can discuss technical questions especially fruitfully, must in all circumstances be regarded as one of his most beautiful works—even if it were advisable. Sometimes one likes just those works less well, when one hears them, from which in a technical, specifically orientated interpretation many things emerge as highly plausible. (Karlheinz Stockhausen, *Reihe*, 2/37.)

When Schoenberg made the attempt to find new laws for the organization of the tonality-free material which he felt was chaotic, he especially wanted to give a musical work the strongest possible coherence by developing a whole movement or work from the same note-series. Webern saw his development in this way: 'Mozart and Haydn had less "thematic exactness" than Beethoven. But they already created space for everything that happened in sonata form: just as the gardener digs the bed in which he plants his flowers. Only in Beethoven was the presentation of musical ideas in the horizontal dimension completed; then there was a reversion, especially in Brahms. In Brahms the independently developed subsidiary parts determine the character of the theme, but in Schoenberg they serve to form relationships in the content of the work.'[1] Webern often used the word 'unity' in his lectures, but gave it a certain mystical meaning, especially when he spoke of 'a deeper unity': 'We want to say "in an entirely new way" what has been said before. Only now can I invent more

[1] *Lectures*, p. 57.

130

freely, everything has a deeper unity. Now for the first time it is possible to compose with free imagination, without restraint—except that of the series. It is paradoxical: full freedom has only become possible through this unexampled control!'[1]

The idea of creating as many relationships as possible now determines the structure of the series more and more. In Opp. 17–20, by using many minor-second relationships in the horizontal as well as the vertical dimension, Webern was clearly trying to ensure the kind of sound which had been characteristic of him since his early works and was recognized as the really constant element in his music. From the Symphony Op. 21 on Webern aims to place the motivic unity in the series itself, at first by laying out its second half as a retrograde of the first half (a relationship which in fact is hardly audible). Already in the series of the Quartet Op. 22 there is a small motivic relationship, between notes 2, 3, 4 and notes 4, 5, 6, which becomes even stronger in that of Op. 25: notes 1, 2, 3; 4, 5, 6; 10, 11, 12. The *ne plus ultra* of this concentration of relationships within the series, or, as Vlad says, of four micro-series which make up the series, is achieved in the Concerto Op. 24: 'Here the idea of serial variation has invaded the detailed structure of the series itself, which reproduces in principle the whole structure of the twelve-note composition. In the course of the whole concerto the systematic and exclusive use of this series, which in its turn is composed of four micro-series, leads of necessity to a constant invention on a single motif of three notes. It is as if the whole sound organism had germinated from this single cell, which constantly reproduces itself in different aspects and relations.'[2]

---

[1] *Lectures*, p. 55. [2] Vlad, *Storia*, p. 125.

Ex. 92

Motif *b* is the retrograde inversion of *a*, motif *c* is the retrograde
of *a* and motif *d* the inversion. The minor second is a typical
feature of the basic motif: it also links *a* and *b* in the series and thus
occurs five times. The motif corresponds to a chord of type IIIa
(see p. 39), which therefore pervades the whole work. But the
motivic relationship produces peculiar identities in transposition:
the motifs are changed over, but within the motifs we get for
instance 3, 2, 1 instead of 1, 2, 3. This is a certain permutation,
but it arises from the layout of the series and is a secondary element: or, to put it better, the layout of the series allows a certain
number of possibilities of permutation to appear, i.e. two of the
six possible permutations on three numbers and four of the twenty-
four possible permutations on four numbers. But Webern did not
arrive at this choice from the possibilities of the notes in the series
changing places by permutation, but through the musical process
of varying motifs by inversion, retrograde and the combination of
both. In his analysis[1] Stockhausen sees the procedure the wrong
way round. He says of bars 1–5: 'On the other hand the internal
sequence of three notes is altered: P1 1 2 3/4 5 6/7 8 9/10 11 12/P2
321/65 4/9 87/12 11 10,' and further, 'the original compositional
unit of 4 × 3 notes perpetually appears in a new order in a quad-

[1] *Melos*, 1953/343.

ruple aspect.' From this he concludes: 'Schoenberg's thematic serial principle is broken. The first variation of the series of 4 × 3 notes, which appeared above in P2, certainly is a transposed retrograde of the original series, but at the same time we have an internal permutation of the three-note group. . . . So the essential element is not an idea chosen for the whole work (theme or motif) but the chosen sequence of pitch, note-values and dynamics. Webern constantly uses this proportion-series in new shapes. Instead of identity there is universal relationship. Development, derivation and variation are replaced by the introduction of a circulating arrangement of notes. . . . The outlook for us: to compose by improvising in a chosen Proportion-field.'

Naturally every composer is free to allow himself to be influenced by Webern's work in the most personal way, and to derive for himself any compositional procedures he likes by analysis. But one must say objectively that it is wrong to ascribe a serial technique to Webern which is based on note-permutation. In essence he did just the same thing as hundreds of composers in the tonal epoch when they changed

Ex. 93

to

Ex. 94

i.e. 'permutating' 3, 1, 5 into 5, 3, 1. Webern had a sufficient knowledge of mathematics to have allowed him, supposing he had worked with permutations, to have discovered those possibilities too which did not arise in the normal process of musical composition. In any case real permutation as a procedure in composition comes not from Webern but from Joseph Schillinger (1895–1943). In the preface to his book *The Schillinger System of Musical Composition* Arnold Shaw and Lyle Dowling say: 'Mathematical theories of combination and permutation serve to reveal all of the possible variations within certain scale patterns.'[1]

Stockhausen's analysis was of particular importance because it formed the conclusion of a ceremony in honour of Webern's seventieth birthday at the Kranichstein Summer School, Darmstadt, in 1953. 'With this, in the year 1953, the new standpoint, the principle of [total] serial composition, was so clearly achieved and so precisely formulated that we, looking back, now have to take up the threads which came together in this new centre,' Karl H. Wörner said regarding this lecture.[2] C. Dahlhaus and R. Stephan[3] have occupied themselves with this analysis and with the attempt, based on errors of thought and perception, to derive from Webern's works the serial treatment of nearly all the elements of composition, and to prove that this kind of compositional procedure is the only one suitable for composition with electronic means. Their basic conclusion runs as follows: 'The relation between music and mathematics has been turned upside down. Although number-proportions and logarithmic correspondences can be found behind the traditional musical system, it does not follow from this that mathematical operations produce musical sense.' The man with the best knowledge of the musical possibilities of electronics, Hermann Heiss, comes to the same conclusion: 'Combination-building, like any form of mathematics, is in itself never capable of producing an artistic utterance.'[4]

The Concerto Op. 24 begins with a three-bar phrase which exposes the basic motif and its variant forms like a motto. The 'answer' follows on the piano in retrograde inversion.

[1] Vol. 1, p. xx.   [2] *Darmst. Beitr.*, 1959/10.
[3] *Eine 'dritte Epoche der Musik'*.   [4] *Musikalische Konbinatorik.*

Ex. 95

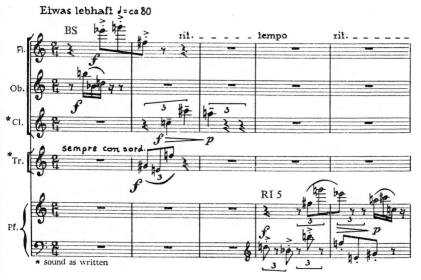

This basic material comes in perpetually new forms, of which these are some of the most characteristic:

Ex. 96

The unity is audible even when the three-note motif is condensed into a chord. (It is well known that the audible comprehension of the coherence between the horizontal and vertical dimensions presents one of the greatest problems in listening to twelve-note serial music and evaluating it from the aesthetic and poetical point of view.) The beginnings of the second and third movements show further developments of the basic motif:

Ex. 97

Op. 24, No. II, 1

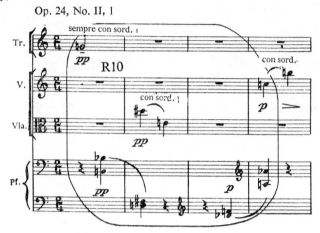

Ex. 98

The whole work is developed from a single three-note motif; Schoenberg's idea of the greatest possible unity is here thought through to its final implications and realized in a composition.

One can approach a work of this kind from several points of view, and the various possibilities of different attitudes can only be explained by the different types of personality. To begin with, the philosophical-speculative type with his general philosophy of life who marvels at organic growth from a germ-cell, speaks of monads and cosmos and sees in a work like Op. 24 a musical correspondence to the Goethean—not to say Goetheanian[1]—idea

---

[1] A reference to the Goetheanum, a 'free high school for spiritual science', established c. 1913 in Dornach, near Basle, by the German theosophist Rudolf Steiner (1861–1925).

of the primeval plant. One cannot altogether deny the justification of such an approach, as Webern's work, especially in his later period, was also very much nourished by such ideas.

The mathematical-engineer type approaches a work like Op. 24 in quite a different way. Perhaps he has read Schillinger's book *The Mathematical Basis of Arts* and finds variations of motifs which in Op. 24 *could* have been arrived at by permutational means, and 'develops' these possibilities further in a logical way. With this he arrives at a mathematically precise procedure, which through a certain aptitude in musical organization can easily be manipulated by a kind of sleight of hand, and so removes those agonies of creation which must have very much afflicted the not so advanced Webern.

Finally, the primarily musical type will be able to appreciate by his ear alone a great deal of Webern's intentions in Op. 24. But even if, following a characteristic of our times, he has a penchant for monothematicism and monomotivicism, he will perhaps not escape the impression, which increases with repeated hearings, than monomotivicism is very near to monotony, and that in this work Webern has not always escaped the danger altogether. The principle of composition, 'It is always something different and at the same time always the same'[1] produces a certain equilibrium which lacks the contrasts from the tension of which a work of art draws its essential force. Is the logical and radical pursuit of a single artistic principle an adequate basis for works of art? In a letter to Křenek of 12 December 1939 Schoenberg answered the question in the negative: 'But the intelligence of the young Americans is really remarkable. I am trying to steer this intelligence into the right paths. They grasp principles marvellously, but want to use these too much "according to principle". And that is wrong in art. That is what divides art from science: in art there should not be principles which have to be used as principles: things are narrowly circumscribed which must remain "wide-open": musical logic does not respond to "if . . . then" but loves to use possibilities denied to it by if . . . then.'

[1] *Lectures*, p. 53.

Das Augenlicht, Op. 26 (1935) for mixed chorus and orchestra

To my daughter Amalie Wallner

> The four-part harmony is made up of three statements of the basic series and one of the inversion . . . Such expressive passages are often to be found in the works of Webern's final period: and the remarkable quality of these works is their combination of extraordinary aural beauty of sound with strict formal control. (Humphrey Searle, *Twentieth Century Counterpoint*, p. 103.)

We are well informed from Webern's letters about the genesis of this work: 'You ask me what I am going to work at: principally, I think, an orchestral work, but more than that I am occupied with the idea of writing a choral work with orchestra on a text of yours!'[1] 'I have already found what I was looking for: "Das Augenlicht" from *Viae Inviae* and have already started work.'[2] ' "Das Augenlicht" is finished.'[3] On 15 October 1935 Webern wrote to the author of his text:

> And so before our next meeting I would like to say something to you on this subject, above all something which I would long have liked to express, and especially at the moment when you asked me what your words meant to me: 'O sea of glances with its surf of tears!'
>
> (It is exactly the middle of the piece and also its dynamic climax.) What an idea! And when in the continuation of this (there immediately follows the greatest musical contrast) you arouse a conception which can only be the inner concept of all that is lovely and pure:
>
> > 'The droplets which it sprays on the blades of your eyelashes are shone upon by the heart and by the sun,'
>
> you create a kind of expression which seems to me the highest: the tears, a drop of water 'shone upon by the heart and the sun': and what makes them flow? No answer is needed.

The highly expressive verses of the poet led to a setting in which Webern is not afraid of romantic passages like:

[1] To H. Jone, 7 February 1935.
[2] To H. Jone, 24 February 1935.
[3] To Humplik and Jone, 17 September 1935.

Ex. 99

In many passages the chorus is written 'note against note', clearly in order to make the text especially clear. But even such bars with their remarkably simple effect are entirely constructed from various forms of the series at different levels:

Ex. 100

This 'strata-arrangement' of the series is the most prominent feature of the writing in Op. 26. Stemming from the expression of the text, the vocal parts rather than the instruments generally have the leading role. So, for instance, in bars 8–19 the series in the choral parts are treated like a cantus firmus, while they are very much split up in the instruments and give the impression of a contrapuntal play around a cantus firmus. Leibowitz speaks of 'intense lyricism' and 'melodic warmth' in regard to the vocal works, but of 'bareness' in respect of the instrumental ones.[1] Webern himself seems to have been conscious of a certain contrast between his instrumental and vocal works: 'I have started my new work already. As I told you, this time it will again be a purely instrumental one. Your texts don't leave me alone, but perhaps it has got to be like that this time.'[2] Very much in

[1] *Schoenberg*, p. 223.   [2] To H. Jone, 15 October 1935.

contrast to a purely vocal period, 1915–26, and an exclusively instrumental one, 1927–30, from 1934 on both categories appear in regular alternation in Webern's works:

Vocal	Instrumental
Op. 23	Op. 24
25, 26	27, 28
29	30
31	32 (unfinished)

Variations, Op. 27 (1936) for piano
To Eduard Steuermann[1]

I   *Sehr mässig*
II *Sehr schnell*
III *Ruhig fliessend*

I have been able to work well. I have already finished one section of my new work. I told you that I was writing something for piano. The finished part is a variation movement: it will become a kind of 'Suite'. I hope I have expressed something with the Variations for which I have had an idea for years. Goethe once said to Eckermann, when the latter spoke enthusiastically about a new poem: 'I have been thinking about it for forty years, after all.' (To Humplik and Jone, 18 July 1936.)

Webern's only piano work is also his most frequently performed composition, and has strongly attracted the analysts because of its relative ease of presentation and perceptibility—but it is not easy to play!

The problem of variation form occupied Webern the whole of his life. As an heir of the great tradition which led through Beethoven, Brahms and Reger into our century, he adopted Schoenberg's ideas of 'developing variation' to an enormous extent, and so variation gradually became the basic principle of his work. 'When studying form one ought really to take variation form as early as possible,'[2] was his view as a teacher; and in con-

---

[1] Eduard Steuermann, a Viennese pianist, pupil of Schoenberg and Busoni, took part in the first performance of *Pierrot Lunaire*. He was a well-known teacher in New York, where he died in 1964.   [2] *Lectures*, p. 58.

versation with Willi Reich he went on: 'The study of the development of variation technique provides a direct approach to serial technique. The relationship to a theme or a series is analogous in both cases. But Schoenberg once said: "The series is more and less than a variation theme." More: because of the stricter relationship of the whole to the series. Less: a series provides fewer possibilities of variation than a theme.'

In the Symphony Op. 21 a theme of melodic importance is formed out of the series, is designated as such and developed in clearly separated variations. All this is missing in Op. 27. Here the series has become the theme, and one might even say that the first appearance of the series is already the first variation as well:[1]

Ex. 101

Op. 27, No. I

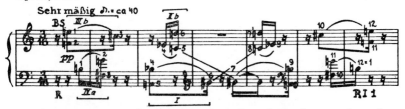

The basic series and its retrograde are heard simultaneously and produce a very complex whole, laid out in mirror form. So, as the two forms of the series cross in bar 4, there is a symmetrical layout round a central axis. This seven-bar group maintains its characteristic stamp by being divided into clearly defined three-note motifs, which considerably facilitate the listener's comprehension of the work when they return in bar 12 and especially from bar 37 onwards. The fact that these motifs are projections of chords of Types IIb, IIIb, I and IVa (see p. 39) shows that the same chord-technique is present in the late works which we have already noted in the first non-tonal works.

Webern's method of variation is shown clearly by the continuation in bars 8–10. Here forms I 2 and RI 1 appear together; they take up only three bars altogether. This compression arises through alteration of rhythmical elements: in the first seven bars

[1] The series is often given wrongly, as in Vlad, *Storia*, p. 126, and Rognoni, *Espressionismo*, p. 204: it is stated correctly in Jelinek, *Anleitung* I, p. 15, and Ogdon, *Series*, p. 79.

the motifs were 5/16 phrases, in bars 8–10 they become 3/16 phrases.

Ex. 102

Ex. 103

In the middle section of the A–B–A form, where the figuration is in strong contrast to that of the outer sections, Webern uses the simultaneous unrolling of two forms of the series in a very interesting way. The handling of the series in the second movement is treated in a very analogous fashion.

Ex. 104

Op. 27, No. II

In his analysis Schnebel has summed up the form of the work as a whole: 'Considered as a whole, the Piano Variations are a broadly laid out work, in which two movements come before the main section of the "Theme and Variations" (the last movement) to prepare for the main part of the work. These contain two different methods of procedure and modes of expression, and real variation can only begin with the synthesis of the two.'[1] The results of Ogdon's attempts to find a kind of tonality in Op. 27 are remarkable.[2] On the basis of the use of linguistic methods he found a symmetrically arranged choice of sound material which shows a similarity to the system of organization which Borris found in Op. 21. Webern's remarks about tonality on the basis of the twelve notes related to one another[3] can perhaps only be properly understood in the light of these discoveries.

As regards the interpretation of the Variations Peter Stadlen,

[1] p. 81.   [2] *Series*, pp. 84 ff.   [3] To Willi Reich, 3 May 1941.

whom Webern mentioned in a letter of 16 October 1937 to Humplik as a 'very talented Viennese pianist', and who is now living in London, has given some information about his work with the composer which goes far beyond the individual opus and is of fundamental importance for the performance of Webern's works. For weeks Webern spent countless hours with Stadlen in order to study the work with him in all its details:

> As he sang and shouted, waved his arms and stamped his foot in an attempt to bring out what he called the meaning of the music I was amazed to see him treat those few scrappy notes as if they were cascades of sound. He kept on referring to the melody which, he said, must be as telling as a spoken sentence. This melody would sometimes reside in the top notes of the right hand and then for some bars be divided between both left and right. It was shaped by an enormous amount of constant rubato and by a most unpredictable distribution of accents. But there were also definite changes of tempo every few bars to mark the beginning of 'a new sentence'. . . . He would occasionally try to indicate the general mood of a piece by comparing the quasi improvisando of the first movement to an intermezzo by Brahms or the Scherzo character of the second to that of the Badinerie of Bach's B minor Overture, of which he said he had thought when composing his piece. But the way this had to be carried out was always firmly fixed in Webern's mind and never in the slightest left to the mood of the moment.[1]

Stadlen gives an impressive example of Webern's demand for considerable, but purposeful use of the pedal from the last movement:
Ex. 105

[1] *Score*, 22/12.

The composer's supposedly pointillistic style appears here in quite a new light. Paul Jacobs too has written interestingly about the use of the pedal in Webern's Variations.[1]

Stadlen also discusses the fact that Webern made so many important demands on the interpreter which he did not put in the score, and the possible reasons for his not doing so. He says: 'However this may be, it appears that an authentic performance of a Webern score is impossible without direct tradition.'

Webern's attitude regarding an analysis of the work for its interpreter was peculiar and very disappointing for the present widespread view of people who over-analyse his works. Stadlen relates:[2] 'Webern never once touched on the serial aspect of his Piano Variations. Even when I asked him, he declined to go into it with me—because, he said, it was important that I should know how the work should be played, not how it was made.'

String Quartet, Op. 28 (1937-8)
To Mrs Elizabeth Sprague Coolidge[3]

I   *Mässig*   *see review in PNM, Spring/Summer 1969*
II   *Gemächlich*   *for unfavorable comments on*
III *Sehr fliessend*   *the following analysis.*

I am on a string quartet. In it perhaps I will especially fulfil the basic principles which you laid down in your letter. How pleased I was to read that! (To H. Jone, 3 February 1937.)

I have come to an important dividing line in my work: the first movement of my new string quartet is finished. (To Humplik–Jone, 2 September 1937.)

A very pleasing postscript has come to a message from America: they want the dedication of a string quartet instead of, as originally, some other kind of chamber music: so this is a splendid solution, as my present work actually is a string quartet! So I do not need to interrupt this, am not pressed for time and can now get it finished without much trouble when it is needed. (To Humplik–Jone, 23 December 1937.)

---

[1] *Domaine musical*, 1954/71.   [2] p. 16.

[3] American patroness of the arts who created the Foundation named after her at the Library of Congress, Washington: since 1925 it has given commissions to composers, including Bartók, Casella, Hindemith, Malipiero, Piston, Prokofiev, Schoenberg (third and fourth quartets) and Stravinsky.

I have just finished another section, the second movement of the quartet which I am writing, and I am going on now to the third one, which will probably be the last. (To Humplik–Jone, 9 February 1938.)

I have worked a great deal in the last few weeks and have finished my string quartet Op. 28. It's now going to America, i.e. the parts go to Kolisch in London. (To Willi Reich, 29 April 1938.)

The string quartet, like all Webern's cyclical works, is based on a single series. Its construction shows a kind of combination of the layout of the series of Opp. 21 and 24. Leibowitz has demonstrated the rich variety of relationships in the series of Op. 28.

Ex. 106

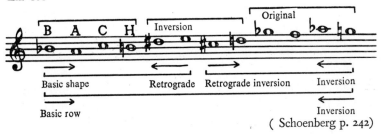

(Schoenberg p. 242)

The series shows a motivic division into four-note groups: the first is B–A–C–H (B flat–A–C–B natural), the second is the inversion of this, and the third the B–A–C–H motif transposed. A further motivic formation divides the series into two groups of six notes: the second half is the retrograde inversion of the first, from which it follows that the inversion of the whole series is identical with the retrograde. So, as in Op. 21, half the forms of the series are excluded, and as in Op. 24 there is considerable motivic identity.

The second and third movements are entirely built on the use of the series in four separate strata:

	Beginning of second movement		Beginning of third movement	
Vl. 1	I	6	BS 6	
Vl. 2	BS	1	I	9
Vla	I	10	BS	
Vlc	BS	9	I	3

But there are also passages in the last movement in which this condensed kind of writing is opened out, and shows a varied presentation of contrasting ideas:

Ex. 107

Op. 28, No.III, 16

A remarkable contrast to such very charming development passages is the stark, angular opening of the first movement, with its two-note motifs in long note-values, in which the series is exposed as if in one part only. One can see how these brief motifs are gradually developed into larger combinations in the course of the movement:

Ex. 108

Op. 28, No. I, 33

and one can certainly agree with Eimert's view of the 'motto-like' character of the beginning of the Quartet: 'In the first sixteen bars of the movement Webern gives a perfect example of his interval technique such as he has hardly shown in any other of his works, in a form almost reduced to a formula. It is as if he were going out of his way to present us with a blueprint of the essence of his interval technique.'[1] Particularly when listening to the work one gets the impression of an organic development from the beginning of the quartet to its last bars. It is remarkable that this organic plan, which one could well believe hovered before the composer's eyes as a basic formal idea *before* the invention of details, was not a part of the original conception of the work. Leibowitz tells us[2] that the order of the movements was originally different (2, 1, 3), and that the Kolisch Quartet had often performed the quartet in this sequence. However, Webern had doubts about beginning with a calm movement and letting two faster ones follow it, although Kolisch pleaded for the original sequence. Finally Webern decided to change the two movements round, which much improved the work. In Leibowitz's analysis, incidentally, which was based on an earlier copy of the work, the second movement comes first.

In connection with Stockhausen's analysis of Op. 24 and its important consequences for post-Webernian methods of composition an interesting detail in the serial technique in the first movement is worth mentioning. After the first exposition of the series in bars 1–6 the following passage occurs:

Ex. 109

Op. 28, No. I.

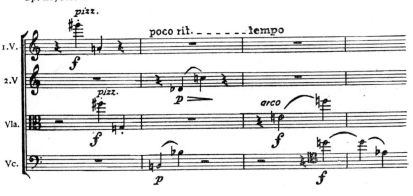

[1] *Reihe*, 2/94.   [2] *Schoenberg*, p. 243.

These note-groups only appear in I 9, but in a different order:
Ex. 110

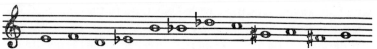

It seems at first as if Webern had used permutational procedure after all. But this is not so in the String Quartet. The peculiarity of the series, that the first four notes, transposed, are identical with the last four, presented a certain problem with regard to the maintenance of intervallic tension. Webern solves it in such a way that in each new entry of the series there is an overlap:

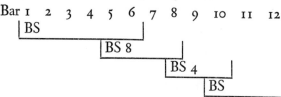

Such a procedure had become normal for one, two or at the most three notes if a retrograde form followed a series in its basic form, i.e. BS–R or I–RI: this was to prevent the same notes following each other too quickly. In Op. 28 the overlapping of four notes prevents the B–A–C–H motif from coming twice in the basic series: basic form and inversion alternate. The series are laid out as follows in the opening bars:

Thus the twelve-note group in Ex. 109 belongs to two different statements of the series.

The Quartet Op. 28 has aroused critical consideration which touches the fundamentals of Webern's compositional procedure: 'In Webern's Piano Variations and the String Quartet Op. 28 the fetichism of the series is predominant. They contain merely single-formed, symmetrical presentations of the marvel of the series. The mysteries of the series cannot console one for the simplification of the music: marvellous intentions, like the fusion

of true polyphony and true sonata form, remain powerless even
if the construction is fully realized, as long as they confine themselves to the mathematical relations in the material and do not
realize themselves in the musical form itself.'[1] Rudolf Stephen
joins in this sequence of ideas: 'The compositional procedure
makes a somewhat rigid and lifeless impression here. Perhaps it
was exactly this restraint in the material which has recently made
Stravinsky become an admirer of Webern's after ignoring him for
almost forty years. In any case the extraordinary differentiation of
sounds, the best element in Webern's art, here appears to be
frozen up.'[2]

First Cantata, Op. 29 (1938/9) for soprano solo,
mixed chorus and orchestra
Text by Hildegard Jone

  I   *Zündender Lichtblitz des Lebens schlug ein*
  II *Kleiner Flügel Ahornsamen schwebst im Winde*
 III *Tönen die seligen Saiten Apolls*

The course of the form of Webern's late works can only be grasped with
the help of Hegelian philosophy. (Dieter Schnebel, *A. v. Webern*, p. 5.)

It is particularly fortunate that, in respect of his last works,
comprehensive statements by Webern have been published in his
letters: these give a valuable insight, not only into the processes
of the composition, but also into the work itself and especially
into Webern's attitude to poetry.

> Now let me tell you as well: I am now setting *Kleiner Flügel
> Ahornsamen schwebst im Winde.* . . . It is meant to become the
> key to a large symphonic cycle for soloist, chorus and orchestra
> which will contain other things of yours: a kind of symphony
> with vocal sections.[3]
>
> It is the first version in score of *Kleiner Flügel Ahornsamen . . .*
> I am convinced that you will be able to see everything from the
> 'picture' which the music presents. But what seems to hover

---

[1] Adorno, *Philosophie*, p. 74.
[2] *Neue Musik*, p. 54.   [3] To H. Jone, 20 January 1938.

149

around in it so freely (*schwebst im Winde*—hovers in the wind)—
perhaps there has never been anything so musically dissolved—
is the result of a strict law and control (the 'little wings' 'already
carry in themselves'—but really, not figuratively—the 'whole
form'. So your words say!)—a control such as perhaps has
never before been the basis of a musical conception. But how
much these words came to meet me!![1]

Meanwhile I have started working on something from the
Distichs! . . . I am fusing three of them into a musical unity.
It will be for chorus and orchestra. And this cycle of movements which I plan will be a cantata, thus exclusively vocal,
on words of yours![2]

The movement from my new work which I told you about
—on a distich of yours—is finished. Now I am writing out
the score. It is a piece for mixed chorus and orchestra. I have
not used the whole text which I thought of originally; the
musical form demanded it differently. There are some purely
instrumental sections, and in the middle your distich *Zündender
Lichtblitz des Lebens* for chorus.[3] . . . I would like to tell you
that the *Chariten* are now finished! The piece needed a lot of
work. In its construction it is a four-part fugue: but to get all
freedom of movement within this fixed form, so that there was
no question of coercion—that was not easy. So that it has also
become something quite different, a scherzo form based on
variations. But still a fugue! Now I am producing the score.
This will take a lot of time—to achieve a sound of a more
varied kind than has ever appeared to me before.[4] . . . but I
was entirely buried in my work: the Cantata Op. 29 is finished.
In its construction it[5] is a four-part double fugue. But subject
and countersubject are related to each other like antecedent and
consequent (period), and elements of the other, horizontal way
of writing also play a part. One could also call it a scherzo,
also variations! But it is still a strict fugue.[6]

I have now finally finished the score of my cantata, i.e. the

[1] To H. Jone, 1939.   [2] To Humplik-Jone, 15 March 1939.
[3] To H. Jone, 14 May 1939.   [4] To Humplik-Jone, 2 December 1939.
[5] The last movement. H.S.   [6] To Willi Reich, 9 December 1939.

last part I have worked at. I have put this section at the end of the cantata after all. Musically this must be the final movement. It was so in my plan, and it has turned out to be so. There is no single musical centre of gravity in this piece. The harmonic construction, resulting from the individual parts, is such that everything remains fluid.[1]

I can tell you that the score of my cantata has gone off to Switzerland—it is possible there will be a performance in Basle. Naturally there is the danger that people will recoil from its great difficulty. But after all, the things I could do with my own chorus in those days![2]

It is remarkable that Webern, whose reputation is that of the extreme opposite to neo-classical mentality, a man who had gone beyond traditional forms, always used familiar formal expressions when he spoke about his own works. These terms were certainly not mere aids to understanding, as he certainly would not have needed to use them in this way when writing to a correspondent like Willi Reich. H. Eimert has taken up a position totally opposed to Webern's when he says in respect of the String Quartet Op. 28: 'Concepts introduced from outside do not help much, and are none the better for being taken from the golden treasury of fugue or sonata form, so as to arrive comfortably at yet another well-loved "synthesis" of the two.'[3] Eimert has also spoken of the overture form of Op. 30 in a similar way.[4] The attempt to find well-known formal schemes in analysing Webern's works is almost always a failure. Expressions like fugue, aria, overture were symbols for basic types of musical construction for Webern, but to him did not mean preconceived moulds such as the neo-classicists tried to fill 'with new content'. Webern saw the fugal element in the third movement as a contrast to the sections in which chords for the voices in strict serial sequences predominated and also to those instrumental sections which have an intermezzo-like character because of being very much split up into motifs and chords. 'The contrast between firm and loose is fundamental.

[1] To Humplik-Jone, 16 January 1940.
[2] To Humplik-Jone, 19 March 1940.　　　[3] *Reihe*, 2/99.　　[4] *Reihe*, 5/7.

The firm quality of the main idea—exposition of the theme!—
is different from that of a codetta. Even in Bach's fugues one can
see this contrast in the episodes,' Webern said in his teaching.[1]
In addition, in the firm formal passages in the third movement
the chorus is supported throughout by the wind, in a way which
is reminiscent of his instrumentation of Bach's *Ricercare* with its
division into motifs.

The first movement is also based on the contrast between 'firm'
choral sections and 'loose' instrumental episodes. The first entry
of the chorus, of which Searle says that it must surely be one of
the most difficult in the whole of music,[2] contains four forms of
the series, in a similar way to Op. 26, but gives the listener the
impression of simple homophony, in which a few rhythmical
deviations give the effect of apparent polyphony:

Ex. 111
Op. 29, No. I, 14

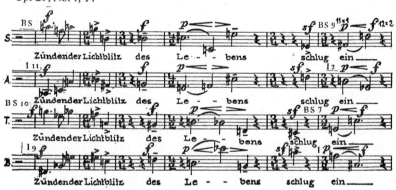

(See Ligeti's exhaustive analysis of these bars).
The series which is the basis of the whole work is constructed
on the model of that of Op. 28:

Ex. 112

Here as there are two groups of six notes which are in the relation

[1] *Lectures*, p. 58.　　[2] *Monthly Musical Record*, 1946/231.

of BS:RI and four three-note motifs with related structures. The
supposition of permutational procedure is even closer here than
in Opp. 24 and 28: Group *b* is a transposed variation (2–1–3) of *a*,
Group *c* is the retrograde inversion of *b*. Together with the
inversions eight forms of the motif appear: four further ones,
which do not arise from the series, are not used. This motif
appears in four separate parts like a motto at the beginning and
in bar 6, and is the starting- and ending-point of four forms of the
series, this time in a looser formation in between:

Ex. 113

These three four-part chords again clearly show how Webern
had developed away from the 'work to rule' of twelve-note orthodoxy: the first and third chords have two notes in common—thus
the third chord is 'impure', contains 'wrong' notes (similarly in
bar 6). Webern had written bars like this starting from a different
conception, in his pre-twelve-note years. After using serial technique for fourteen years he could allow himself chord-sequences
of this kind again, because he had long risen above narrow
pedantic rules, and serial polyphony was more important to him
than the construction of correct twelve-note groups. Eimert[1] goes
so far as to say: 'Webern's thought stands in the sharpest contrast

[1] *Reihe*, 2/36.

to automatic twelve-note writing, to dispose of which all his creative counter-forces had to be brought into play.' In this connection it is interesting that bars 6 and 7 of the third movement show an entirely undodecaphonic accumulation of three F sharps which belong to three different forms of the series.

Variations for Orchestra Op. 30, (1940)
To Werner Reinhart

When a first performance is on the way, especially an orchestral one one thinks naïvely above all: How will it sound? And one enjoys it in advance, equally naïvely!—But the performance must give the right sensory impression. If you revel in sounds then you are doing it right, conductors! (To Willi Reich, 4 September 1942.)

There are extensive remarks by Webern regarding this work in letters to Willi Reich which are especially interesting because Webern divides them to a certain extent into (*a*) replies to quite general objections and (*b*) an analysis for a specialist. He worked on this piece for about a year.

'I have started a new work: this time it will be instrumental.'[1]

I am again at my own work, which I had had to interrupt for so many weeks. It will be a purely instrumental work: a very variegated one, but on a basis of strict coherence.'[2]

Also I have worked without interruption and can tell you, that I am almost at the end of my present labours. As I told you before, it is a purely instrumental affair, for orchestra: variations. A fairly long, self-sufficient piece.'[3]

I have needed such a long time to get to the end of my orchestral variations. I suspected that it might be difficult . . . but I didn't know it would take so much time. I have sat at it for weeks and weeks. And now, I think, something quite simple and perhaps obvious has come out of it. The piece lasts about a quarter of an hour,[4] in very quick tempo almost throughout, but sometimes with the effect of a sostenuto. In general form it is supposed to be a kind of overture, as planned, but based on variations. . . . There is the synthesis again: the presentation is

[1] To Humplik-Jone, 16 January 1940.   [2] To H. Jone, 1 August 1940.
[3] To H. Jone, 20 December 1940.
[4] The performance in the complete recording takes 5 min. 40 sec. H.S.

'horizontal' as to form, 'vertical' in everything else. Basically my
overture is an 'Adagio' form, but the reprise of the main theme
comes in the form of a development, so this element is there too.'[1]

I would like to say to you in a few words something about
the work which you could perhaps use effectively to counter
possible objections and which may clarify the whole thing.
So please understand me: I would like to speak quite differently
to you yourself about the work on another occasion. Isn't it
true that when one first sees this score one wants to say: There's
'nothing in it'!!! This is because one doesn't see the many,
many notes which one is accustomed to see, in Richard Strauss,
etc. Quite right! But now we come to the most important point:
we can say basically, here . . . is a different *style*. Yes, but what
sort of a style? It doesn't look like a score of the pre-Wagnerian
period, e.g. Beethoven, nor does it look like Bach. Should we
go still further back? Yes, but—in those days there weren't any
orchestral scores! So what sort of style? I think, a new one. . . .
Now I would like to explain the piece from the score. Some
important things in a few words: the theme of the variations
goes as far as the first double bar: it is conceived as a period, but
has an 'introductory' character. Six variations follow, each up to
the next double bar. The first so to speak brings the main theme
of the overture (which is in Andante form) fully exposed: the
second is the bridge-passage, the third the second subject, the
fourth the recapitulation of the main theme—for it is an Andante
form!—but in a *developing* manner: the fifth repeats the manner of
the introduction and transition and leads to the Coda, the sixth
variation. Everything in the piece is derived from the two
phrases stated in the first two bars by double bass and oboe!
But this is still further reduced, as the second phrase, in the oboe,
is already retrograde in itself: the second two notes are the cancrizan of the first two, but in augmentation rhythmically. Then
the first (double bass) phrase follows again in the trombone, but
in diminution! And in cancrizan as to motifs and intervals.
That's how my series is built up, formed from these three
groups of four notes. But the succession of the motifs joins in

[1] To Willi Reich, 3 March 1941.

this retrograde effect, though using augmentations and diminutions! These two kinds of variation lead almost exclusively to the ideas of the different variations: this means, motivic alteration only takes place within these limits, if at all. But by changing the centre of gravity in all possible ways within these two phrases something new in time-signature, character etc. keeps on appearing. . . . '[1]

The series of Op. 30 is even richer in micro-structures than its predecessors in Webern's works:

Ex. 114

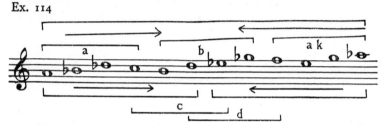

Again the second half is the retrograde inversion of the first. From this it follows that the last four notes are the retrograde inversion of motif *a*, and motif *b* consists in itself of two two-note motifs with the same inter-relationship. There are two further motifs in the series, overlapping with each other and with the former ones: *c* = *a*R transposed, and *d* = *a* transposed. From this layout, with its rich variety of relationships, four-note motifs and

Ex. 115   Op. 30, 1

four-note chords arise which are characteristic of the whole work.

In the first variation Webern again adopts a procedure which occupied him during his whole life, the creation of 'strata' of sound. What the listener hears here as melody plus chordal accompaniment is exactly constructed according to serial technique, but the 'law' is so ingeniously handled that in truth 'something quite simple and perhaps obvious has come out of it'.

Ex. 116   Op. 30, 21

In the fourth variation the minor second is the constructive principle: the series, which appear in four levels with a short distance of entry between them, are a semitone apart from each other in pitch I (| 6, | 7, | 8, | 9). H. Searle says[1] in connection with his analysis of this work: 'The brief technical analysis above has been inserted for the benefit of those who like to know how the wheels go round, but it is not, of course, necessary to grasp all the structural ingenuities in order to appreciate or enjoy the music, the mere sound of which must be enchanting. It is one of Webern's clearest and most attractive works.'[2]

[1] *Monthly Musical Record*, 1946/231.
[2] I had not heard the work at the time of writing the article. The first performance of the Variations took place at Winterthur in 1943 under Scherchen, and Webern was able to be present (*Translator's note*).

Second Cantata, Op. 31 (1941–3) for soprano and bass soli, mixed
chorus and orchestra

Text by Hildegard Jone

I *Sehr lebhaft*
 Bass solo and orchestra
 Schweigt auch die Welt
II *Sehr verhalten*
 Bass solo and orchestra
 Sehr tiefverhalten innerst Leben
III *Sehr bewegt*
 Soprano solo, three-part women's chorus and orchestra
 Schöpfen aus Brunnen des Himmels
IV *Sehr lebhaft*
 Soprano solo and orchestra
 Leichteste Bürden der Bäume
V *Sehr mässig*
 Soprano solo, 4-part mixed chorus, solo violin and orchestra
 Freundselig ist das Wort
VI *Sehr fliessend*
 Four-part mixed chorus and orchestra
 Gelockert aus dem Schosse

Alban Berg once said in conversation that Anton Webern's time would
not come for a hundred years: then they would play his music in the way
people read poems of Novalis and Hölderlin today . . . because more than
any other art 'extreme' lyricism needs time to unfold, and so it always
appears as 'out of its time': densely concealed in the chrysalis of strangeness
and unintelligibility, which keep too early light from it, in order not to
endanger its inner growth. (Th. W. Adorno, Lecture on Südwestfunk,
Baden-Baden, 21 April 1932.)

Many passages in Webern's letters tell us about the genesis of
this work and the composer's attitude to its shape. It is interesting
to see how Webern to some extent started from the end, backwards, so that its final shape remained open for a long time: 'I
very much believe that with your poem *Freundselig ist das Wort*
something new has come to me.'[1] Webern took this central text,

---

[1] To H. Jone, 11 March 1941.

around which the work took shape, from an unpublished collection of Hildegard Jone's:

Blessed is the Word,
that draws us to it asking for our love,
'be not afraid, it is I',
consoles us through the darkness,
which is all around us,
when we are at peace.
What other power can there be among us, but the Word?
Because it died on the Cross we must follow it,
in all the bitterness of tears our sighing follows it.
Yet when it sounds once more in the morning hours,
we all turn to it gladly and know we have been called.
Blessed is the Word.
And when you know that it knows everything of you,
then you know it: then it pains you more deeply than death,
when a cloud of bitter hatred,
the mother of tears, comes between you and it
and freezes everything.

After the completion of the first number the problems of the shape of the whole work began:

. . . I have been entirely taken up with my work (Second Cantata Op. 31) and still am. The first piece in a new choral work, with soloists and orchestra—it may well go beyond the scope of a cantata: that's my plan anyway—this first piece is finished and already written down in score. . . . In form it is introductory, a recitative! But this section is constructed in a way such as perhaps none of the 'Netherlanders' ever thought of: it was perhaps the most difficult task which I have ever had to fulfil, from this point of view! For the basis is a four-part canon of the most complicated kind. The way it is carried out, I think, was only possible on the basis of the law of the series. . . . I have read in Plato that 'Nomos' (law) was also the term for 'tune' (melody). So the melody which the soprano solo sings in my piece as the introduction (recitative) is supposed to be the law (Nomos) for everything that follows![1]

[1] To Willi Reich, 23 August 1941.

Freundselig is almost finished . . . I was lucky enough to achieve in it, I think, an, I might almost say, entirely new style of writing: for from a purely polyphonic basis I have arrived at what is as good as the most contrasted kind of writing.[1]

The question of economy in the instrumentation, and also some questions in the composition, have held me up longer than I had expected. It has become a kind of 'Aria' for soprano solo, chorus and obbligato violin solo . . . with orchestra. You ask about the 'shape': at the central point come the words 'Because it died on the Cross'. Everything that went before repeats itself backwards after this. 'Repeats' itself: 'all the shapes are similar and none is the same as another: and so the chorus hints at a secret law, a sacred riddle'. You know this line of Goethe's! (*Metamorphose.*) The fact that it was just those words which formed the middle of the musical shape came entirely by itself, and could not have been otherwise! The end was difficult: 'bitter hatred'—'cold': in the warmth and 'friendly blessedness' of your words!!! and so in the music we hear here like a breath: 'we all turn to it gladly'. . . . But even this I see now for the first time—and it came unintentionally. . . . And now the other texts for my new work! For I am planning a large-scale work which will keep me busy for a long, long time.[2]

The further growth of the work can be followed in the letters to Humplik and Jone of 4 September 1942 and 11 February 1943, to Willi Reich of 6 August 1943 and Hildegard Jone of 11 October 1943. Finally on 28 January 1944 Webern was able to tell Hildegard Jone that the Cantata had found its final shape and that with it his work on it was finished. He compares the individual numbers to the sections of the Mass and says: 'Now look at the sequence: hasn't it basically become a "Missa brevis"?'

The basic series, as derived from the first entry of the soloist in the first movement, is:

Ex. 117

[1] To H. Jone, 3 June 1942.   [2] To H. Jone, 25 July 1942.

Ex. 118

Op. 31, No. VI

This time again a series without 'inner construction' for a work
based on a text. Six-note chords, formed from segments of the
series, punctuate the recitative-like introductory movement. The
final chorale provides a complete contrast to this loose formation.
(See Example 118 on previous page.) The score looks like that
of one of the Netherlanders, not only because of the long note-
values, but also because of the 'mensural' differences in the
barring. Webern specially pointed this out to Reich: 'I believe
you will be astonished by the look of this score. Long note values,
but very flowing tempo.'[1] 'What will you say about it? If for instance you look at the score of the sixth movement?'[2] However,
the archaic effect which one might expect from looking at the
score is more or less annulled through the quick tempo and the
actual sound. One should take note of the 'a cappella instrumentation' and the fact that Webern allows the three verses to be
exactly repeated. In this, towards the end of his creative life,
he moved as far as possible from the aesthetic principles of his
youthful years.

In the choral part of the fifth movement we find the sliding
harmonies which can also sometimes be seen in earlier works:

Ex. 119

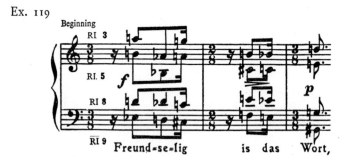

This arises from the use of various simultaneous transpositions
of the same form of the series.

[1] 4 September 1942.   [2] 6 May 1944.

THE ARRANGEMENTS

Webern's work as an arranger ranges from piano scores to creative rebuilding. On the lowest level is his bread-and-butter work which he often complained about in his letters, though he was certainly thankful to his publishers, Universal Edition, for offering it to him at times of the greatest financial difficulty. Webern, as a conscientious musician, probably spent more trouble on this type of work than was perhaps necessary. Quicker colleagues probably earned their money more easily.

Among the piano scores—but on the higher level of service to a friend and of works which interested him very much—were the arrangements for voice and piano of the Six Orchestral Songs Op. 8 of Schoenberg. The songs were written in 1904: the piano scores appeared in print in 1911. They are carried out with great care, and the attempt to reproduce as much as possible of the original has led in places to high demands on the performer, both from the pianistic point of view and because of the professionalism which Webern showed in reproducing the original. Rufer tells us[1] that there are piano scores by Schoenberg himself of several of these songs. These are probably piano versions made before the orchestration, and we must assume that they have not been printed because of the considerable alterations made to the songs in the orchestral version.

The arrangement of Schoenberg's Five Orchestral Pieces Op. 16 for two pianos is more than a piano reduction: it stands to the original rather in the same relation as the independent version for two pianos of Brahms' Haydn Variations does to the orchestral work. Certain adaptations of the original were necessary here. Incidentally, Schoenberg himself arranged the work for chamber orchestra (single woodwind, piano, harmonium and string quartet, the so-called 'Paris version') when he urgently needed arrangements of this kind for the performances of the 'Society for Private Musical Performances in Vienna' which he founded in 1919. This society, in which Webern acted as master of performances, i.e. he helped to prepare the material and directed the

[1] *The Works of Arnold Schoenberg*, p. 27.

preliminary rehearsals, was always short of money and could only afford large combinations very rarely. But smaller groups of the kind described above were sufficient for the 'workshop' character of the work of the society which Schoenberg aimed at. Comparing the original with the arrangement, one is first struck by Schoenberg's relatively transparent and clearly defined orchestral writing, which considerably helped the transcription.[1] But where Webern had to leave something out, i.e. to make a choice, and especially where alterations became necessary, every adaptation is done with so much tact and recreative insight that the arrangement of Schoenberg's Op. 16 can rank as a model for work of this kind.

Performances given by the Society were also responsible for the arrangement of Schoenberg's Chamber Symphony for fifteen solo instruments Op. 9, which Webern reduced to a combination consisting of violin, cello, flute (or second violin), clarinet (or viola) and piano. Schoenberg had begun an arrangement of it in 1907 for some unnamed instruments, and it is possible that Webern took over this work as early as the year of its first performance, 1907, to relieve his teacher. All these arrangements gave Webern a unique opportunity of getting to know the works fundamentally. The 'High School of Copying and Arrangement', which was practically the only means of education for a composer like Bach, still had its uses in the twentieth century.

Paul Stefan speaks of another arrangement of this kind in his Schoenberg essay.[2] On 14 January 1910 Schoenberg's Piano Pieces Op. 11 and his George Songs Op. 15, were given their first performances at the *Verein für Kunst und Kultur* (Society for Art and Culture), followed by the first part of the *Gurrelieder* in a piano arrangement made by Webern. This performance, which took place before the instrumentation had been finished, had a great success with the public, and perhaps moved Schoenberg to take up the work again: it was finished in the following year. The printed piano score of the *Gurrelieder*, by the way, was made by Berg.

The orchestration of Six German Dances, op. posth., by Schubert leads us into the very different world of the 'arrange-

---

[1] Both versions are published by Peters.   [2] p . 37.

ments': Webern orchestrated them from a piano score for double woodwind, two horns and strings. These pieces were written in 1824 and only discovered in 1931: they were published by Universal Edition in the original version. Webern's arrangement was commissioned by the publisher, and was carried out with such an exact knowledge of Schubert's orchestration that they could almost have come from his own hand.

Webern made an arrangement of his own Five Movements for String Quartet Op. 5 for string orchestra. He mentions this for the first time in a letter to Humplik: 'In the last few weeks I have been busy with an arrangement of my first string quartet for string orchestra. But I am very proud of what I have achieved in it.'[1] In the following year Willi Reich reported on the first performance: 'The composer's own arrangement of his Op. 5 for string orchestra also had its first performance in America. This arrangement is not just a transcription of the quartet score for string orchestra, but, keeping true to the notes of the thematic framework, it achieves an instrumental expansion into an entirely new body of sound. This new version, which in places is divided into fifteen parts, opens up an entirely new direction for the technique of arrangement and will certainly show the way for all attempts of this kind in future.'[2]

After comparing the two versions one will perhaps not entirely agree with Reich's somewhat over-enthusiastic judgment. Webern had an exact knowledge of the capabilities of the string orchestra, and Berg was often glad to ask his advice on questions of instrumentation. He has simply transcribed the work, just as an excellent musician would do in such a case, but there was little opportunity for fundamental revolutions in the technique of arrangement. Nos. 3 and 4 are transcribed practically without alteration: in other pieces the new forces are split up and the musical substances loosened thereby. Especially in Nos. 1 and 5, Webern subdivides each individual group of instruments and notates them on two staves. Through using one to three solo violins, and in addition solo viola, solo cello and solo double bass, as well as occasionally using the first desk alone, he obtains

[1] 4 March 1929.　　[2] *Die Musik*, 1930/815.

additional possibilities of refinement. He is able to intensify the sound-expression by giving violin passages which would have to be played on the less tonally productive middle strings to the more suitable register of the solo viola or the rich-sounding tenor register of the solo cello (No. 1 bar 27, No. 2 bar 5, No. 4 bar 2). By using the manifold possibilities of the string orchestra it is possible to divide single melody lines between two or more instruments. Thus the long-drawn-out viola melody of No. 2 is divided like a dialogue between solo cello and solo viola. This splitting-up is perhaps the most personal characteristic of the new version of Op. 5, and it is worth remembering in this connection that it was written after Webern had composed the Symphony Op. 21. Passages like No. 1 bars 14f. and No. 3 bar 7 are especially characteristic of this 'unravelling' of the sound. This pointillistic technique seems to oppose the tendency towards 'closed' sounds, as for instance No. 1, from bar 38 on, shows. The passage in thirds and sixths, played in the original by viola and cello, is given to the two groups of cellos in the new version. In a similar way the last crotchet of bar 54 is played by solo cello and cellos in four parts. Practical experience with the string quartet no doubt led to the simplification of the chords in harmonics: more suitable division between the instruments allowed artificial harmonics to be replaced by natural ones in several places. Purely practical considerations, as well as those of sonority, also led to violin passages which are difficult to play or especially difficult in intonation to be given to one or two solo violins, as in No. 1 bars 2–3, bars 38–41 and especially No. 5 bars 20–1.

Webern was still very attached to the second version of the quartet pieces in later years. On 23 February 1944 he wrote to Willi Reich:

The score of my string orchestra arrangement of Op. 5 will be sent to you as soon as possible. It should be played by as large a body of strings as possible so that the constant regroupings (tutti, halves, soli) can make a good contrast with each other in sound. It has become something quite new! As regards sound! I can only say: what a lot the conductor gentlemen are missing!—I am very glad that you now want to take up the cudgels for it! I think people will be astonished! . . .

But his view, especially as regards the comparison with the first version, is not entirely shared by critics today. Hinner Bauch says: 'Webern's five Quartet Pieces Op. 5, played here in the not very advantageous version for string orchestra. . . .'[1] And H. H. Stuckenschmidt explains further:

> In the augmented reproduction (which however Webern himself made) one can certainly feel the string quartet spirit of the original form. The expiring pianissimi, fleeting sighs and starkly flashing chords are not suited to the big apparatus, even if they are played with the delicacy of chamber music.[2]

The real central piece among Webern's arrangements is the *Ricercare a 6 voci* from the Musical Offering (1747) of J. S. Bach on a theme of Frederick the Great. As everybody knows, Bach's six-part score of this piece has no instrumental indications. The idea of arranging it may have been suggested by Schoenberg, who orchestrated two chorale preludes of Bach in 1921, a Bach organ work, the Prelude and Fugue in E flat, in 1928 and arranged a Handel concerto grosso for string quartet and small orchestra in 1933. But it must be pointed out that Schoenberg used works whose realization in sound had been exactly laid down by the composer, while Bach had left the combination needed for the Ricercar open. The arrangement was made in 1934/5. On 10 December 1934 Webern wrote to Hildegard Jone: 'I am working day and night on the Bach Fugue,' and on 7 February 1935: 'I was still busy with the Bach Fugue up to the day before yesterday: I've thought over many points again and again!' On 20 March 1935 he was able to tell Josef Humplik: '. . . on 25 April I am conducting in London. There I am doing the first performance of my Bach Fugue, as well as two works of mine and a classical symphony.' Webern's method of handling Bach can be shown by comparison of the subject and answer in the original and the arrangement:

[1] *Melos*, 1959/119.   [2] *Melos*, 1959/121.

Ex. 120

poco allarg. _ _ _ _ t.

The Arrangements

The theme, which is divided by a rest into two long phrases, was split up by Webern into seven motifs, divided between four instruments. The counterpoint (bar 9f.) to it is heard in a dialogue between second violin and solo viola, and the string colour is contrasted with the woodwind group which plays the theme. The whole work is scored in this way, very transparently and with the clarity of chamber music: only in some passages, especially towards the end, are there orchestral effects with part-writing in octaves. About its performance Webern wrote in a very interesting letter to Hermann Scherchen:[1]

> I am very glad that you are performing 'my' (I think I can call it that) Bach Fugue on the BBC! . . . Now as regards your question: the 'rubato' you ask me about means that I think of this bar of the fugue theme, together with all the counterpoints which come with it later, as played with movement each time: accel.-rit., finally merging into the 'poco allargando' of the last notes of the theme. I feel this part of the theme, this chromatic progression from G to B, as essentially different in character from the first five notes, which I think of as very steady, almost stiff (that means in strict tempo: the tempo must be set by them) and which, according to my idea, find an equivalent in character in the last five notes. To describe it more accurately, I intend the 'rubato' thus: from G through F sharp to F is quicker, then holding back a little on the E flat (accent on the harp) and then again rubato on the trombone phrase (including the tied E flat of the horn, i.e. the crotchet rest in the trombone —that is bar 6). By the way from G to E flat there are also five notes, and, if you count the E flat twice (in the sense of a link!) in the intrinsic rendering of the theme, this first crotchet in bar 6 (the tied E flat in the horn and the simultaneous crotchet rest in the trombone) is heavily stressed as a dividing point, an end and a beginning (it is scored thus): so that if one counts this E flat twice one again has five notes, from E flat to B. So the form seems to me: five notes, then 4 + 1 and 1 + 4 which is twice five, and finally five notes again!

[1] 1 January 1938, *Reihe*, 2/25.

And these middle (as it were) twice five notes, being so to speak the actual centre of the structure, I feel to be quite different in character from the beginning and from the end: the latter leads back with its poco allargando to the stiffness of the beginning, now appearing in the answer. Dynamically that means that you must make a very clear difference between the pp of the first five notes and the p of the middle ones! And in the last five notes go back to the pp with the molto dim. (▷). I hope I have made myself clear. Naturally I must also add that the theme throughout must not appear disintegrated. My orchestration tries (here I am speaking of the whole work) merely to reveal the motivic coherence. That was not always easy. Beyond that it will show my feeling for the character of the piece: what music it is! The ultimate object of my bold undertaking was to make it available at last by trying to show in my arrangement my view of the work! Yes, isn't it worth while awaking what still sleeps here in the seclusion of Bach's own abstract presentation and so for most people remains either completely unknown or at least unapproachable?

Webern's arrangement was given its first German performance by Scherchen at the Kranichstein Summer School, Darmstadt, in 1954, together with Schoenberg's orchestration of the Bach organ work. Since then people have been very much divided by 'Webern's Bach Ricercar' at all its performances and the most opposite views have clashed head-on. There were already violent arguments in Darmstadt in 1954, and what Heinz Joachim reported in *Melos*[1] regarding the Schoenberg arrangement also applied to the Ricercar:

A few days ago the Darmstadt Stadthalle was the scene of an argument in which the discussion of basic problems of the summer course came to life once more. Hermann Scherchen played Schoenberg's orchestral arrangement of Bach's organ prelude and fugue in E flat, which was commissioned by an American conductor and actually ingeniously worked out, though it was very far from any attempt to be faithful to a

[1] 1954/259.

historical style. Even before the performance was over it aroused the loud opposition of a youthful purist. This hiss of protest was all the more distressing as the impression arose that insufficient knowledge of the work was a factor in the untimely moment of this demonstration. It was also distressing to learn that it had been suggested beforehand to those taking part in the course that this arrangement of Schoenberg's was the only possible way of making Bach come alive today. Behind such an extremely authoritarian form of 'indoctrination' there lies a fanaticism of exclusivity against which young people have a right to defend themselves if they do not want the approach to music to be purely one-sided.

Contrasting views can also be found in books, e.g. Adorno:[1] 'The Bach arrangements by Schoenberg and Webern, which convert the most minute motivic relationships of the composition into relationships of colour, thus realizing them for the first time, would not have been possible without the twelve-note technique'; Leibowitz[2] on the arrangements (which are after all fundamentally different from each other) of the Schubert dances and the Ricercar: 'These two scores are realizations of an absolute perfection . . . these two orchestrations show how far the genius of Webern—so eccentric at first sight—has been able to maintain contact with the great, the true musical tradition of the European West.' Willi Reich[3] on the complete recording: 'A model example of such a successful attempt can be found in Band 2 on Side 8: the six-part Ricercar in the orchestration made by Webern in 1935; here the masterly contrapuntal structure was already given: to fill its abstract framework with the most living expression was the problem which Webern resolved in the most sublime manner.' Boulez:[4] 'Webern, who made a magnificent orchestration of the great fugue in six parts from the "Musical Offering", would have been happier if he had not been followed by many disciples of the "twelve-note school" who felt themselves obliged in their turn to dress up Bach or Mozart in tinsel which is not only tawdry

[1] *Philosophie*, p. 57.   [2] *Schoenberg*, p. 251.
[3] *Schweizerische Musikzeitung* 1960/322.   [4] *Contrepoints*, VII/73.

but clumsily applied.' When Boulez wrote these lines, did he anticipate that a young composer would undertake to make a new version of the 'Art of Fugue', an undertaking of which Heinz-Klaus Metzger says[1] that the author 'almost thinks out further what had been begun in Webern's orchestral analysis of the six-part Ricercata'? The term 'analysis' is also found in Rudolf Stephan:[2] 'The thematic evolution is now clearly audible, and at the same time it is clear why Webern chose to arrange Bach: here he could show that the conventional method of performance, which rejoices in being "true to the work", in fact depreciates the work in that it sacrifices musical reality to the ideology of "linear counterpoint" (Kurth). But the orchestration of the theme of this great fugue shows how Webern brings the "line" to life in his construction. In fact we here have the realization in sound of an analysis.' Very much in opposition to such remarks are critics such as Helmut Schmidt-Garré:[3] 'Webern tries in the *Ricercata* to make the structure of the Bach fugue clear by a constantly changing division of individual motifs between various instruments, but in this he nevertheless comes considerably close to a variegated romantic colouring,' or Heinrich Lindlar:[4] 'The effect of the "exchange of sounds" on the linear work of the cantor of St Thomas's is that of softening, not concentration. A remarkable, if dubious, meeting of minds.' Critics who wish to be neutral, but remain on the heights of the terminology of the time, say something like: 'Webern has introduced tone-colour into the structure,' and Craft in the introduction to the recording, referring to passages like bars 13 and 14, speaks of a structural use of pizzicato. To complete this survey of the various points of view, Nestler says:[5] 'The arrangements of Bach's music . . . show that it is possible to impose new problems on old music, as long as they are immanent in the music. In this way old music provides the new problems with their justification.' But H. H. Stuckenschmidt has probably said the deciding word:[6]

The pointillist process, i.e. the division of a melody between

---

[1] *Reihe*, 4/78. [2] *D.Univ.Zeitung* 1956, Vol. 11, No. 13/14.
[3] *Melos*, 1958/131. [4] *Musica*, 1960/32. [5] *Der Stil*, p. 30.
[6] *Schöpfer*, p. 201.

several instruments which appear to form the links in a chain, has been built up into a method by Webern's followers. Webern himself used it in his orchestration of the six-part fugue. The endeavour to achieve the strongest possible accentuation allows the motifs to pass from one instrument to another, so that the aesthetic impression of a 'plane' of colour is produced, in the same way that the neo-impressionist painters Paul Signac and Georges Seurat used a larger number of dots in close proximity. But with Webern there is not so much an impressionistic urge for expression behind this as a strong will to construct and dissect.

This sense of 'dissection' is perhaps one of the chief characteristics of the development of Webern's style, and it already clearly showed itself in such an expressedly polyphonic work as the Song Op. 15 No. 5. In fact in the Bach arrangement we are confronted with an 'orchestrated analysis' or an 'analytical orchestration'. We possess a sufficient number of fugues or fugal expositions orchestrated by Bach himself and know his own method of doing this; Webern naturally knew this perfectly well. But if he still let himself in for such a 'bold undertaking', he did it with creative mastery and transformed the Bach work into one of his own. The phrase 'my Bach Fugue' has a deeper meaning here: in the arrangement Webern has almost created an original work. Anyone who listens to the Ricercar as a work of Bach's is bound to be disappointed. In Bach the motifs are the foundation stones of the long line: they fulfil their function in just being there without obtruding. Webern teaches analysis with the searchlight of tone-colour. So the motifs acquire a life of their own at the expense of the line. Webern is not even afraid of dividing up a motif; the fact that the trumpet and harp are not allowed to finish their motif E flat–D–C after bar 8 is symptomatic of the 'dissecting' position he had reached.

Webern's arrangement does not really demonstrate 'romantic colouring' nor the 'spirit of bringing up to date'.[1] It seems much more a result of that heightened analytical thinking which has

[1] Uhde, *Prisma*, p. 129.

characterized or expressed European attitudes to music more and
more, since the turn of the century, and its development has taken
place at the expense of the tendency towards synthesis. A direct
line runs from Riemann through Schenker to those present-day
'score-gazers', who, with a more and more 'refined' analytical
technique, have reached the point of counting the individual notes
and arranging them in tables, as their ultimate exercise. This kind
of analytical thought has influenced the process of composition
more strongly than is generally realized. Perhaps the Bach Ricercar gave such critics of Webern their most productive starting-
point. It is remarkable and characteristic that this aspect has so far
been missed by the anti-Webernites.

WEBERN'S PERSONALITY AS
REFLECTED IN HIS WORKS

Now the whole question is this: . . . How far can our freedom go? This freedom can go as far as the artist's feeling can reach. (Wassily Kandinsky, *Über das Geistige in der Kunst*, p. 117.)

When Hugo Wolf was asked for an autobiographical sketch, he replied: 'My name is Hugo Wolf and I was born in 1860. Everything else you can find out from my works.' If one investigates the gradual growth of Webern's works one can get a deep insight into the formation of his style, but cannot learn 'everything else' from them. Musical analysis has limits. But perhaps one can look a little beyond these limits if one studies all that is known about Webern's personality and its changes, and if one tries to see this picture of a personality in conjunction with the results of studying his works.

When in 1902, the year of the first performance of Debussy's *Pelléas et Mélisande*, Webern left the safe atmosphere of his parents' house and the somewhat constricted spiritual life of his home town Klagenfurt in order to begin his studies for a career in Vienna—which together with Paris and Berlin was then one of the musical capitals of the world—there was already the seed of important developments for the future in the music of the turn of the century, in Debussy, Strauss, Reger and Mahler. But at this time, when autonomous experiments as a possibility of discovering new stylistic methods were more or less unknown, everything new in works of art or at least in conscious artistic production took place on the foundation of a well-tried tradition. It was Webern's task to grow up in this tradition, to learn to master its tools and to absorb its rich profusion of masterpieces. If he chose the study of musicology as a means to this end, he certainly did not do this with the feeling of being a musician who was constricted in advance. Perhaps his parents' wish for him to win an academic degree fitted in with his own ideas, but it was his own way of thinking which was decisive, for it led him to a scientifically exact grasp of the material of music. At a time when the study of musicology was not yet so specialized as it is today, it was customary for the more intelligent musicians in Vienna to undertake a double course of study at conservatoire and university. A large number of leading Austrian musicians had enjoyed a complete education in musicology; this was normally completed without writing a thesis. But Webern undertook these studies with great intensity, and took over part of Guido Adler's enormous research project, which started from his work on the Tridentine Codices, namely the editing of the second part of Heinrich Isaac's *Choralis Constantinus*. Thus he acquired an exact knowledge of the technique of the writing of the so-called Netherlands school, and after his youthful Wagner experience his getting to know Isaac and the masters of his time had a very definite effect on Webern. This essential component of his musical thinking was very much overlaid for a time by his study with Schoenberg, and from 1907 on by his direct participation in the revolutionary musical developments of the time. After Op. 2 canonic writing and occupation with the problems of polyphony almost disappear from his works. With Op. 15 No. 5 the 'Netherlands' components again begin to have their effect, and they are exposed completely in 1924 with the Canons Op. 16. It is interesting that this work is very near in time-relationship to some important 'turning-point' works: Stravinsky, Octet (1922–3), Piano Concerto (1923–4): Hindemith, *Marienleben* (1923): Schoenberg, Suite Op. 25 (1921–3), Wind Quintet Op. 26 (1923–4). In Webern's change of style to Op. 21 (1928), with the four-part canon at the beginning of the symphony, the models of vocal polyphony are more and more clearly traceable and finally led to the remarkable last movement of Op. 31, the appearance of which in the score was commented on by Webern himself. From remarks he made at that time, especially in the lectures, and also in his letters, one can see the part played by Netherlands musical methods in Webern's musical and spiritual conception and also how it entered more and more into a remarkable symbiosis with twelve-note mechanics and even strongly pushed back these latter elements.

Webern's meeting with Schoenberg in 1904 decided his development as a composer. Schoenberg's unique aptitude for teaching can perhaps be explained by the fact that in essentials he was self-taught; he came to music relatively late after a career in commerce and had to forge his own tools of composition by hard work after his spiritual development had already progressed quite far. The lessons, which he gave with real passion, even if in his later years he complained of the time he lost by them, did give him the possibility of continually examining and strengthening his own powers. The opening sentence of the preface to his *Harmonielehre* ('I have learnt this book from my pupils') was certainly more than a consciously shocking paradox, for '. . . the teacher must have the courage to make a fool of himself. He must not show himself as the infallible person who knows everything and never makes a mistake, but as the untiring person who is always seeking and perhaps sometimes finding.'[1] As a result, from the teacher-pupil relationship of Schoenberg and Webern there soon developed a bond of friendship which was based on common searchings and aspirations. The strictness of Schoenberg's teaching, about which Berg among others has written in detail, must have been very sympathetic to Webern's liking for taut self-discipline. A curious situation must have arisen from the fact that Schoenberg was openly 'anti-historical' and once remarked, with a shade of mockery, 'I have never read a history of music.' In a lecture[2] which deals with the creation of the twelve-note method, Webern refers to the origin of some details of the handling of the series: 'Now the analogy still has to be developed, starting from the Netherlanders: the basic set, the sequence of the twelve notes, can give rise to variants. . . .' We can assume that the musicologist Webern's references to the compositional techniques of the fifteenth and sixteenth centuries had a strong influence on Schoenberg and his pupils relatively early.

Schoenberg's fascinating personality deeply impressed Webern and Berg. 'All his pupils became attached to their teacher for

[1] *Harmonielehre*, p. v.   [2] p. 41.

ever,' say Paul Stefan.[1] An exchange of letters with and about Hanns Eisler shows how radically the master demanded complete subordination in spiritual and idealistic questions.[2] The climate of hate in which Schoenberg lived in Vienna when Webern and Berg were his pupils allowed him to become an uncompromising martyr for his ideas in the eyes of his followers and led to a kind of community of gain and loss. Stuckenschmidt says:[3]

> The antipathy shown to him on all sides was compensated for by the faithful and devoted support accorded to him by his pupils and followers, by their unconditional faith in him which at times seemed to regard any criticism of their master as blasphemy. . . . In these years in Vienna Schoenberg's life was a constant battle against all sorts of difficulties, against material privations and against defamatory campaigns on the artistic and intellectual level. The joint effects of material difficulties, self-defence, struggle for existence, and veneration by his pupils thus resulted in an unique atmosphere: and it was not easy for the novice to find his place in the hierarchical circle around this man.

Webern, as much as Berg, was especially disposed to such unconditional devotion and faithfulness to the final limits as the result of his own nature. It is characteristic that in the 1925 Carnival number of the *Anbruch*, in the cast list of a 'Mystical Europa Revue', in which Schoenberg is included as 'The Voice of the Master', 'Herr Berg' is given as 'First Officer of the Bodyguard' and 'Herr Webern' as 'Second Officer of the Bodyguard'.

The experiences with the Viennese public, or, rather of the well-organized anti-Schoenberg clique, bound Webern even more firmly to Schoenberg at the very moment when he was presenting his first works to the public. So at an early stage he became the eternal Schoenberg pupil for large sections of the Press and public: his name was almost always mentioned in connection with that of his master. This existence in his master's shadow even as a composer became a fixed concept which has only gradually been demolished after exhaustive study of Schoenberg's and Webern's

[1] *Schoenberg*, p. 91.   [2] *Letters*, Nos. 90–92.   [3] *Schoenberg*, p. 93.

works. A few quotations will show how far views differ on this point. In the appendix to the Insel edition of Schoenberg's Op. 15 Adorno says of the 14th song: 'The boldest and most advanced of all . . . its influence on his successors cannot be exaggerated: the whole of Webern stems from it.' Leibowitz, who unfortunately saw Webern one-sidedly, from the viewpoint of the Master, goes much further: 'However it is only with the Symphony Op. 21 that Webern's originality entirely comes to fruition. Up till then he had hardly written a page which—perhaps with a certain exaggeration—could not have been written by his master.'[1] There have been strong protests against such a one-sided point of view. Herbert Eimert:[2] 'with or without exaggeration, this amounts to making blindness the principle of seeing! Even in the early Op. 9 not a bar could possibly have been written by Schoenberg.' Henri Pousseur:[3] 'That would be an opportunity to make a basic differentiation of the poetic qualities of master and pupil, and to realize the individuality of Webern's innovations. A glance at one of his earlier works, e.g. the pieces Op. 5, strikingly shows his emancipation from Schoenberg's atonality: it would make clear the precise extent to which the latter stimulated his speculative powers and sensibilities.' Eimert's and Pousseur's views are unconditionally confirmed musicologically. Rudolf Stephan says:

> Webern's early works, even if entirely valid from all points of view, belong to the stylistic area of certain definite works of his former teacher. The force of these models is preserved in the pupil's compositions. But one cannot say that Webern and Berg merely used Schoenberg's innovations in their own way: it seems far more true that they were joint conquerors of the new musical territory. So long as this question has not been cleared up, we cannot without further thought ascribe to Schoenberg as the originator every compositional moment which can be found both in Schoenberg and in Webern.[4]

And Wolf Isensee, in an analytical comparison of three orchestral works of Schoenberg, Berg and Webern, arrives at the following view of Webern:

[1] *Schoenberg*, p. 210.　　[2] *Reihe*, 2/32.　　[3] *Reihe*, 2/60.　　[4] *A. von Webern.*

His personal style was, if not fully developed, so much stronger in definition, so that Schoenberg was never a mere teacher for him, but the whole period of lessons provided more of a series of mutual stimulations in which Schoenberg was certainly the provider of ideas, but Webern only took from these whatever made the further development of his personal style possible. His works remain more and more isolated from those of his two friends, even if completely understood by them.[1]

Finally Webern himself said in a lecture[2] 'We (!) didn't create the new law ourselves: it overwhelmingly forced itself on us.'

It seems that in Webern, who took up all the problems which interested his teacher and thought them out further, a strong *reservatio mentalis* was at work at the moment of creative activity, which made it possible for him to go his own way as a composer in spite of complete spiritual devotion to Schoenberg. In later years this led to a clear difference of opinion, even on fundamental matters. A letter of Schoenberg's to Kolisch of 27 July 1932 on the question of analysis makes this clear: 'But the aesthetic qualities are not disclosed by it, or if so, only incidentally. I cannot warn often enough against over-estimating these analyses, as they only lead to what I have always fought against, the knowledge of how it is *made*: while I have always helped to find out what it *is*! I have tried to make Wiesengrund[3] understand this many times, and Berg and Webern too. But they don't believe me.'

Webern's encounter with Schoenberg was not in itself so important for his development as a composer, but it was the moment in time of this meeting and Schoenberg's stage of development at that time which mattered. 'What I'm telling you here is really my life-story. This whole upheaval started just when I began to compose,'[4] Webern later said about this time. In artistic creation which is essentially based on considerable identity of personal development and the development of the style of the time, in cases where someone is influenced by someone else who is in a very different state of development this can lead to the destruction

[1] *A. Schoenberg's Op. 16*, p. 58.   [2] p. 54.
[3] Wiesengrund is T. W. Adorno.   [4] *Lectures*, p. 44.

of the organic spiritual growth of one partner. In contrast to the
positive element of fundamental and decisive stimulation, he faces
the danger of not living through his own evolution but the
spiritual revolution of someone else, not of creating his own next
work but the next work of the person who stimulates him.
Webern's path from Op. 1 to Op. 5, which took just two years,
reflects these dangers. Schoenberg's restlessness of spirit created
an atmosphere among his pupils and followers which came very
near to the 'permanent revolution' expressly demanded by Varèse.[1]
Webern formulated this intellectual position in a lecture[2]: 'In fact
we have to break new ground with each work: each work is
something different, something new. Look at Schoenberg! Max
Reger certainly developed too, as a man develops between his
fifteenth year and his fortieth: but stylistically there were no
changes: he could reel off fifty works in the same style. We find
it really impossible to repeat anything.' Stuckenschmidt referred
to basic relations in the history of the mind when he said: 'Freud
denounced the compulsion to repeat things as a neurotic symp-
tom.'[3] 'Only what has not been said before is worth saying'[4] was
the artistic slogan of the Master's circle. This is understandable
when one thinks of the productions of the followers of Wagner and
the rigidly academic successors of Brahms, who dominated the
musical life of Austria and Germany in the first decade of this
century. But it can lead to a neurotic fear of 'falling back into
tradition' and to a convulsive searching around at all costs. 'My
pupils know what it is that matters—seeking' Schoenberg said in the
Harmonielehre.[5] 'And a wrong idea found through honest seeking
still ranks higher than the careful safety of someone who guards
against this because he thinks he has knowledge—knowledge
without having sought it himself!'[6] Helmut Kirchmeyer has
pointed out the fundamental difference from Stravinsky from this
exact point: [7] 'After all it only depends on the result, the finished
work.'[8]

---

[1] Boulez has recently coined the parallel idea of 'permanent discovery',
Darmstädter Beiträge, 1960/27.   [2] p. 45.   [3] *Schoenberg*, p. 134.
[4] Schoenberg.   [5] p. vi.   [6] p. 2.
[7] *Stravinsky*, p. 30 f.   [8] Th. Stravinsky, *I. Stravinsky*, p. 13 f.

There was a deep and essential difference between Webern and Berg in their relations to Schoenberg: Webern was more stable and logical, Berg softer and more open to impressions. These characteristics led in a remarkable way to quite opposite consequences in relation to Schoenberg. Once Webern took over Schoenberg's world of ideas he developed it further without compromise; Berg, who wrote *Wozzeck* against the strong advice of the Master, was more bound by tradition and also used the twelve-note method with a very personal kind of treatment which was strongly permeated by tonal relations.

It was Webern's lack of compromise which has created an entirely false picture of the composer for the last fifteen years or so; people like to think of him as a revolutionary ascetic and an anti-romantic extremist. But Webern gave Stuckenschmidt the impression of a calm, introvert person 'of the type of a kindly young country priest',[1] and Roberto Gerhard, the Catalan composer now living in England who was a pupil of Schoenberg and Webern in Vienna, says: '. . . it was never clear to me to what extent Webern's lifelong association with the Austrian socialist party may have rested on actual political convictions. His background, I suppose, could have been described as "gut bürgerlich", the same as Schoenberg's though a little more upper-middle-class.'[2] The political connection of Webern, of whom it was related that he said his evening prayers on his knees every night,[3] to a party which forty years before had been almost officially free-thinking was hardly based on political-philosophical convictions. Artistic work for and with workers was certainly the result of a basically Christian standpoint which Webern took very seriously and this had bad results for him in 1934 in Catholic political circles.

Webern was averse to all radicalism, especially in musical questions—apart from his own work. He felt himself strong enough in the creative field to be able to acknowledge all that was great and beautiful in music without complexes or envy. Frederick Deutsch Dorian tells of studying conducting with Webern:[4]

[1] *Schoenberg*, p. 33.   [2] *Score*, 28/26.   [3] Goléa, *Esthétique*, p. 66.
[4] *Melos*, 1960/101.

His love of Beethoven was a decisive pointer for us young students too. The conducting course began with the first symphony and reached its peak with the study of *Fidelio* ... his love of Mozart, which shows itself in Webern's own scores. He adored the *Entführung* and interpreted Mozart's early style with extraordinary acuteness. . . . The study of the repertoire was naturally influenced by the necessities of the operatic profession. Webern knew the routine repertoire perfectly. He knew every cut, every unmarked cadenza, and in the comic operas every theatrical joke, whether good or bad. One may be surprised to know that *Zar und Zimmermann* was one of his favourite operas. If he was in good humour he would sing Lortzing's arias and ensembles. He recreated the musical Biedermeier style in a gay, immediately present form. And he performed comic scenes for us with unexpected dramatic gifts and pantomimic élan ... On other occasions Webern spoke of Strauss with great respect. '*Salome* will last,' he prophesied of this revolutionary score. For making a synthesis of art music and popular music Webern's undivided respect was given to Johann Strauss alone. . . . Apart from opera his analyses of vocal music made the deepest impression: his interpretation of the *Winterreise* was unforgettable. Yet no one who know Webern's lyrical writing will be astonished by this preference in taste.

On 5 November 1933 Webern wrote to J. Humplik: 'I wish you could come to my concert tonight: I have a fine programme: Schubert, *Rosamunde*; my arrangement of the Schubert Dances, and the Brahms Serenade in D major. All delightful, friendly music. How beautiful the Brahms is!' And on the BBC Webern once conducted a programme which included some Strauss waltzes.

Not only letters to Hildegard Jone[1] confirm that Webern was seriously interested in operatic plans: Dorian once asked him about this precise point and got the reply: 'If I live long enough and find a good text.'[2]

Dorian has given full details of Webern as a teacher (Schoen-

---

[1] Nos. 13 and 17.   [2] *Melos*, 1960/10.

berg once described him as the 'most passionate and intensive teacher'): 'Webern presented to all of us who came to study with him the model of a life dedicated to art. His incomparable virtues had a strengthening effect. They gave weapons to the character of the young people who surrounded him. We learnt from his example that the greatest achievements came from sacrifices.' Webern's theoretical instruction was based on strict writing in the style of the old vocal polyphony. It

> . . . consisted of concentrated, exactly balanced solutions of the play of thought from one lesson to another. He was not impressed by any kind of merely industrious work . . . he was not interested in routine. Easy craftsmanship he regarded as basically a handicap. For Webern all music must pass the test of true expression and honest invention. Without these there was no technique. Clearly his method sometimes put the patience of the immature novices to the test. When one is very young one wants to get on quickly. . . . But Webern held the reins inexorably tightly. He taught not only strict writing but the still stricter discipline of being able to wait, of patience for the maturing of meaningful work. So his method of teaching reflected his own creative process, his search for valuable material and the unflinching testing of this on the scales of the most refined feeling for style. . . . Webern tried to awake the sense of historical thinking in his pupils and to support their feeling for style objectively by means of historical knowledge. So he helped me too to find the profound value and intellectual compensation of musicological work. He showed me the way to the combination of the practical and historical disciplines of music in the same way as he had learnt them himself as a student.

In this connection Dorian quotes a very characteristic remark of Webern's: 'You will understand my advice later. Meanwhile you must believe me.'

Dorian says of Webern as a conductor (he often referred to virtuoso conductors as 'dancers' and refused to conduct without a stick because it 'reminded one of the jazz style'): 'All effects were interior ones, even the dramatic climaxes. Everything was an immediate expression of the experiences of the heart and nerves. Everything was dematerialized in the service of the spiritual idea and the highest quality of playing.' It is clear that a conductor who concentrated so much on the essence of the music had no chance of making a 'success' with the public and critics. A review by Erich Steinhard[1] of the tenth International Music Festival in Vienna, in which he speaks of Webern's 'Biedermeier-like gestures' is characteristic. His foreign tours as a conductor as well as his conducting work in Vienna were not caused by a general appreciation of his capabilities but by the special insight of individuals, such as the BBC producer Edward Clark or the Viennese cultural politician D. J. Bach. Adorno wrote of a concert on Frankfurt Radio[2] that Webern had performed Mozart's G minor symphony and Mahler's *Kindertotenlieder* 'as only a great composer can conduct them' and asked the question: 'When will the conductor Webern obtain the position which is due to him?' In 1936 Webern's sensitivity almost led to a catastrophe at an international music festival in Barcelona. Still under the shadow of Berg's death (Christmas 1935), he was asked to conduct the first performance of Berg's last completed work, the Violin Concerto. Of the three rehearsals at his disposal Webern used two for the first eight bars, so that Scherchen had to step in and save the performance on a single rehearsal. Two years later[3] Webern wrote to Scherchen about 'the unhappy days in Barcelona': 'To think that absolutely no one understood me then! No one understood how I was so soon after Berg's death, and that I was simply not up to the emotions aroused by the task of giving the first performance of his last work—so soon after the event! Right up to the last moment I hoped to be able to stand it. But it didn't work out!'[4]

Schoenberg in a letter to Webern described the latter's nature briefly but accurately: 'I am very glad that your diagnosis was so satisfactory. The most important thing is to have no real illness in any organ. One cannot wish for more. And everything else will

[1] *Auftakt*, 1932/187.
[2] *Die Musik*, 1930/308.   [3] 1 January 1938.   [4] *Reihe*, 2/19.

be satisfactory with some treatment and care. You ask where all
these symptoms come from. I believe (it sounds old-fashioned,
but I must say it, and with the old-fashioned expression which
one used to use for it) they come from your spirit! I think you get
too excited about everything. Whether you conduct, take a
rehearsal, have to carry something through, suffer criticism, and
who knows what else—you always put too much heart into it.'[1]
The remark about Webern's sensitivity to criticism is interesting.
To say that Webern avoided publicity, 'cut the connection
between his work and the public' and wrote a kind of 'music
against everybody'[2] is another part of the Webern legend which
can be contradicted not only by his continual efforts to get performances but also by some letters of Schoenberg's. 'It is a pity
that you weren't able to do Webern's songs. He will certainly
have been very disappointed, for you know that he takes things
of this kind very badly and always draws conclusions from them,'
he wrote on 1 February 1931 to Heinrich Jalowetz, and on
16 March 1930 from Hollywood to Hermann Scherchen: 'Thank
you for sending me the programme of your International Festival.
It's certainly a big affair, and if I miss anything it is Webern. I
should be unhappy if he were always left on one side (as I was
once) and so had further reasons for bitterness.'

The Webern of the 'lyrical geometry in which it is not feeling
that works up form but form that leads one to feel',[3] who was
'not intoxicated by any daemonism or euphoria in the content
but summoning up form as a regulated phenomenon out of the
inaudible world of structural quantity-relations',[4] also belongs
to the legend. Of Mahler's seventh symphony Webern said: 'It
sounds of nothing but love, love, love.'[5] And he clearly and precisely indicated the way in which he wanted to see his own work in
a letter to Humplik-Jone[6]: 'What you say about me, dear Frau
Jone, (see p. 126), really describes for the first time the content of
what I am aiming to express and so makes me indescribably happy.
For however valuable it is to know the technical side, i.e. the
presentation, exactly, how much one longs for a word about what

---

[1] Berlin, 12 August 1932.   [2] Stuckenschmidt.   [3] Eimert, *Reihe*, 2/35.
[4] Eimert, *Reihe*, 2/31   [5] To. H. Jone, 21 April 1934.   [6] 4 March 1934.

is presented itself, to hear what it *gives* to another person. And so your words, and yours, dear Humplik, pleased me beyond words! They are so lovely that I have to read them over and over again, and they truly warm me!' To eliminate the discrepancy between the authentic portrait of Webern and later Webern interpretation the only possibility is to assume that the composer somehow lived in parallel with the 'real Webern'. Stravinsky put it in this way:[1] 'All this goes back to Webern, who understood the whole problem of variable density—such a remarkable fact that I would very much like to know if Webern himself knew who Webern was?' And Herbert Eimert said: 'We do not know from any utterance of Webern's that he had an inkling of his own situation and significance as a composer.'[2] But Webern's letters from the last years of his life to Willi Reich[3] prove the contrary. One example: 'That's how it's always been in the music of the masters!—Whether I shall bring it off as they did, only God knows, but at least I have recognized what is involved'![4] Cesar Bresgen, who saw Webern frequently during the months after the end of the war, tells us: 'He was convinced that others would follow him on his path. . . . In the last part of his life (how long he had done this earlier I do not know) he had worked out an unequivocal theory to serve for the future, i.e. it bore within itself all consequences, practical use, further development etc. He was convinced of the rightness of his thoughts and knew that one day he would be understood in the widest sense.'[5]

The consequences of Austria's two fatal years, 1934 and 1938, hit Webern very hard.

In 1934 Webern retired into private life as the result of political events, gave up his work as conductor and confined himself to teaching. In 1938, when Austria became National Socialist, he lost his teaching work too and lived almost only for composition. The loneliness which was always present in his music also surrounded his personal life like a vacuum. Finally Webern was in tragic isolation even in the midst of his

---

[1] *Melos* 1958/290.   [2] *Reihe*, 2/36.   [3] *Lectures*, pp. 58–66.   [4] p. 63.
[5] *In Memoriam.*

nearest relations. The man whom he admired above everybody, Schoenberg, was in America, and contact with him more or less ceased during the war. Alban Berg, his companion and friend, had died in 1935.[1]

But it is remarkable that the feeling of inner loneliness is expressed relatively early in his letters. On 30 December 1929 he wrote to Humplik: 'It becomes more and more lonely around one in this world. And more and more difficult!' Anxiety about a general decline in culture and the feeling of a personal responsibility which was becoming more difficult all the time made a deep impression on Webern: '. . . it is getting worse and worse in the world, especially in the field of the arts. And our task becomes greater and greater.'[2] 'The more terrible it becomes, the more our task becomes responsible.'[3] The emigration of many friends and supporters in 1938 in fact left Webern behind in hopeless isolation. 'As he no longer met any productive people, he was certainly more tempted into mathematical speculations, which provided a lonely man with the illusion of cosmic nature,' says Adorno,[4] and Stuckenschmidt enlarges on this:[5] 'In these late years of his life a religious-mystical character, which had already appeared in his sacred songs and Latin canons of 1917 and 1922, deepened in Webern and led him to the eccentric philosophical lyricism of Hildegard Jone. The vocal works of his last years were written to texts of this woman, who was also a close friend.' The number-speculations which Adorno alludes to are also found in his letters. On 11 February 1943 Webern writes: 'But above all I would like to tell you, dear Hildegard, the most beautiful thing I have discovered in connection with the setting of your poem —that, with the exception of the last (fourth) stanza (which in connection with the ending of the work from the musical point of view appears self-evident) each of the three previous stanzas contains the same number of syllables (16)! So that in my note-series at *Farben, Farbenschimmer, Farbige* and in the third stanza, correspondingly, *das Aug mehr bindet,* and also in the defining

---

[1] Stuckenschmidt, *Schöpfer*, p. 196.
[2] To H. Jone, 27 September 1930.   [3] To J. Humplik, 20 February 1934.
[4] *Klangfiguren*, p. 178.   [5] *Schöpfer*, p. 196.

phrases *so lang, wenn nachts, wenn nichts* and in the fourth stanza (as it were as a fulfilment) *tritt das Bewegende* I reach the *same* place each time!!!! Now think: what a correspondence this is musically!!!!' But already on 11 March 1931 he was writing about the series of Op. 24 to H. Jone:

> I have found a series—that is the twelve notes—which shows very far-going relationships in itself among the 12 notes. Perhaps it is something like the famous old saying:

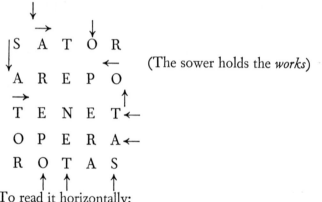

(The sower holds the *works*)

To read it horizontally:
So: Sator opera (mirror-form of arepo)
    tenet, tenet
    opera sator (mirror-form of rotas)
In addition vertically: down from above: upwards: down, up (that is tenet twice): down, up. Then vertically again: begin from bottom right: up, down, etc.

In reading such passages one remembers that very many extra-musical ideas have played a part in modern music. Satie began as a Rosicrucian, and wrote a ballet with a dedication 'To the almighty, radiant and perpetual indivisibility of the three Persons of the Triune' and later founded a sect of his own, *Église Métropolitaine d'Art de Jésus Conducteur*.[1] The theosophist Helena Blavatsky had a clear influence on Scriabin and Schoenberg. The former invented the 'mystical' chord and left behind sketches for a mystery which was to combine the capacities of the indivi-

[1] Stuckenschmidt, *Schöpfer*, pp. 42 ff.

190

PERSONALITY AS REFLECTED IN HIS WORKS

dual arts in a synthesis. Schoenberg, whose unfinished oratorio
Die Jakobsleiter is claimed by the theosophists,[1] dreamed, in
overcoming the different musical species, of a kind of earthly
sexlessness with a fulfilment in the spiritual world.[2] He felt himself
to be 'merely the mouthpiece of an idea'.[3] Hauer started from
Goethe's Theory of Colours, introduced ideas from Eastern
philosophy into the creation of his theory of music teaching and
finally ended up with the 'world builder', whose perfectly finished
absolute music, 'this godlike father-tongue', we should strive to
learn.[4] Herzfeld says of the propagator of athematic composition
and quarter-tone music: 'Hába has given himself over more and
more to the teaching of Rudolf Steiner,'[5] and Wörner speaks of
the 'theologization of music in Messiaen.'[6]

Thus towards the end of his life Webern's mystical tendencies
led to a kind of 'Meta-music' which did not need to be written
down on paper and realized in sound. Bresgen says of this: 'It is
highly improbable that Webern worked at any piece of music
on paper in those last months of his life in Mittersill: in any case
there is no one to whom he spoke about it. On the other hand
one could often see Webern in most stimulating work, which
consisted of drawing with pencil and compasses on a poor quality
table or on a wooden board. I well remember his system of lines,
in which could be seen geometrical figures or fixed points with
markings. Once—it was the middle of August 1945—Webern
said on one of my visits that he had just finished some work which
had occupied him a great deal. He had completely organized a
piece, i.e. he had fixed all the notes in it in respect of their pitch
(sound) and also their duration in time. I cannot remember the
series, but I remember Webern's remark about "time fulfilled".
With this graphic plan on the table Webern regarded the real
work as completed. More than once he made the assertion that
he would never wish to hear his piece (played by musicians).
He said that the work "sounds by itself"—he himself could "hear
it right through"—it was enough for him that the piece was now

[1] Stuckenschmidt, *Schöpfer*, p. 75.   [2] Vlad, *Storia*, p. 36.
[3] Interview in America, 1933.   [4] Pfrogner, *Die Zwölfordnung*, p. 231.
[5] *Musica nova*, p. 273.   [6] *Darmstädter Beiträge*, 1959/11.

finished in itself: "the sound is always there"—"a performance would not bring it out as perfectly as it had already become sound in himself". Apart from this Webern was convinced that what he had done was no private or arbitrary step; he said "one will hear this music as if it had always been, it will be like a morning breeze, a liberation . . . in fifty years one will find it obvious, children will understand it and sing it".'

In a composition which was fixed in its layout and organized throughout in its presentation, of which the existence in the spiritual world was enough for him towards the end of his life, Webern saw something like an organically grown product of nature. His real desire during the whole of his life was to penetrate the mysteries of growth and formation in nature. On 1 August 1919 he wrote from Mürzzuschlag in Styria to Alban Berg: 'I have been to the Hochschwab. It was glorious: because it is not sport to me, nor amusement, but something quite different: a search for the highest, for whatever in nature corresponds to those things on which I would wish to model myself, which I would gladly have within me. And how fruitful my trip was! The deep valleys with their mountain pines and mysterious plants—these above all are very near to me. But not because they are so "beautiful". It is not the beautiful landscape, the beautiful flowers in the usual romantic sense that move me. My object is the deep, bottomless, inexhaustible in all, and especially in these manifestations of nature. I love all nature, but most of all that which is found in the mountains. For a start I want to progress in the purely physical knowledge of all these phenomena. That is why I always carry my botany book with me and always look for any writings which can help to explain all that. This physical reality contains all the miracles. Research, observing physical nature is the highest metaphysic for me.'[1] And Bresgen says: 'One saw the man who had grown lonely, whom no one there knew, chiefly on walks in the high mountain country round Mittersill, which had still remained quite primeval. Webern was often absorbed in the contemplation of plants which he saw on the way. Once we spoke for a long time about the nature of plants, in the wood

[1] *Reihe*, 2/17.

above the castle of Mittersill. This was caused by some curious mushrooms, whose enigmatic nature gripped me in a similar way. In the plant Webern saw splendid, perfect nature in all ways: he studied the creative forces which worked in it. The organic element, the form of existence organized to the last degree always occupied him anew. Through Webern's whole work that characteristic leads to plant life: therefore knowledge of it gives many keys to the understanding of the master.'

THE AFTERMATH

In a hurly-burly where everything tries to acquire prestige as quickly and strongly as possible, where the loud volume of bluff has become more important than the content and form of the product, the creative type who is shy and withdrawn into himself has a very small chance of attracting notice and breaking through. But the laws of art are different from those of life. The maxim of Chinese philosophy that the softest overcomes the hardest applies here. Voices which were so quiet that they could hardly be made audible showed themselves to be the most penetrating: they sounded forth when one had long forgotten the loud-speakers which drowned everything. (H. H. Stuckenschmidt, 'Anton von Webern', in *Schöpfer der Neuen Musik*, p. 192.)

The tension between intervals is not of this world and cannot be manufactured in an artificial way. (Hans Werner Henze, *Gefahren in der Neuen Musik*.)

Silent, modest, unobtrusive and little noticed, as Webern was as a man—so he remained as a composer during his life. His professional colleagues and friends in Vienna esteemed him as an excellent musician, but people hardly took any notice of his works, or mildly ridiculed them at the most. The reputation of his works abroad too was small: the few performances, mostly at music festivals, were either failures or did not have any important results. Only a few faithful followers like Adorno, Reich and Stein spoke and wrote in support of Webern, and only a few interpreters, the chief of whom was Kolisch, took on themselves the thankless task of performing his works. As Webern retired more and more from musical life he gradually disappeared from the consciousness of a public opinion which had regarded him at the highest a marginal figure, surrounded by debate, in Schoenberg's circle. Webern's death remained generally unnoticed.

In the situation immediately after the war the cult of Webern at the Kranichstein Summer School in Darmstadt may perhaps serve as a barometer of the gradually increasing estimation of the composer. It is characteristic that in the first two years, 1946 and 1947, no Webern was performed. As late as 1948 Peter Stadlen gave the first German performance of the Piano Variations Op. 27, which had been written in 1936, and the songs Op. 4 followed in 1949. But in 1953, the year of the celebration of his seventieth birthday, a more extensive cult of Webern began, with the performance of seven works. In 1948 Leibowitz had held a course on Schoenberg's twelve-note method in Germany for the first time and had thus led the way to the introduction of the young composers to Webern's works. Among his Paris pupils were Henze and Stockhausen as well as Boulez. Leibowitz, though argued about as regards his twelve-note orthodoxy, rendered a historic service by being the first to examine Webern's work on a broad basis and to set down the results of this examination in some important publications. If there have been attacks on Leibowitz in this book, this is only because in some works of a compilatory character on the music of our time (and up to now there has been astonishingly little research into the sources) many of his mistakes have been taken over without correction and have been and are being spread further.

Stockhausen[1] has given an impressive account of the exciting experience of the first year of the 'discovery' of Webern: 'The first encounter with Webern's music was unforgettable. One's mind runs back to the days when copies of Webern scores were handed on from one person to the other, when a shared passion for his music caused friendships to be sealed. Since then the circle around Webern has grown ever wider. After the war one could hear the first concerts only with difficulty in which here and there, in between marketable pieces, one of his short compositions was tucked away—at some exclusive music festival or every few months about midnight on the radio.' We know of Boulez that a very mediocre performance of Webern's Symphony Op. 21 was a revelation for him and led him to make a thorough study of Webern's works. If one had asked the generation of twenty- or twenty-five-year-olds at that time what drew them so much to Webern they would hardly have been able to give a definite

[1] *Reihe*, 2/37.

answer. Perhaps it was the lack of rhetoric, the terse language, the concise reduction of the means of expression in many of the late works which fascinated disillusioned youth whose spiritual awakening had come in the horrible last years of the war, youth which was trying painfully to find itself for the first time in a new spiritual atmosphere.

In the narrower professional sphere, about 1948 composers began to adopt the twelve-note method, which in Germany, after long years of being banned, had become a symbol of spiritual freedom in musical creation. This process naturally started with the works of Schoenberg. But the younger musicians quickly showed a certain aversion, especially to Schoenberg's habits of expression. They quickly saw in the 'grand old man' of modern music a late romantic burdened with the style of *art nouveau* and expressionism, with the content of whose works one could not begin anything very new. This aversion led to a critical attitude even to his technical methods of composition. 'One can say that, starting from 1951, classical serial teaching, founded on the technique and style of Schoenberg, had been left behind at Darmstadt,' says Goléa.[1] They felt it as a fragile element in Schoenberg's work that, although he had given powerful impulses to the organization of the sound-element of his time, he remained imprisoned by tradition in the rhythmic field and especially in thematic and motivic working. From the point of view of a homogeneous development of all 'parameters'—this term was used for the first time by Schillinger in his work on the theory of music and then adapted by Meyer-Eppler for Germany and became a fashionable term for a young generation which did not know its a-musical origin—Webern appeared as more modern, and his music as more pregnant for the future. When Schoenberg died in 1951, Boulez made the often-quoted remark 'Schoenberg is dead', which in France meant no more than a variation of the traditional cry 'The King is dead, long live the King', but had a 'shocking' effect outside France. The old twelve-note guard had been angry with the young generation for the very rapid deposition of the 'master' and the dialectically underpinned turning to the 'pupil': especially

[1] *Rencontres avec Pierre Boulez*, p. 77.

because it was suggested that people were linking themselves to a Webern who had in fact never existed. This is typical of all 'turning movements' of this kind which shoot beyond the target and devalue the past from a one-sided and extreme point of view. Stockhausen said about this: 'We have been accused of doing violence to Webern's music by reading into it something which is not there at all. This objection is comprehensible if one tries to grasp its reasoning and its premises. But if Webern is now being seen by other musicians in other ways, this heralds a change in thinking that one should also make an attempt to understand. There is not one interpretation but as many as there are points of view.'[1] Though his first sentences are justified, his last one is wrong. There are also false interpretations, and not everyone who 'looks at' a Webern score thereby acquires the right of twisting the facts written down in it or reading things into Webern's work which are not there at all. Reich speaks in the foreword to Webern's lectures[2] in connection with the new image of Webern of a 'free fantasy'. And in 1960 Nicolas Ruwet demanded a fundamental revision of the falsified picture of Webern: 'Above all one must study Webern's works again. For a long time all studies of Webern's work, even those which incontestably contributed a good deal to the understanding of him, started from an interested point of view, if I may say so. People saw Webern as the creator of a new world and were inclined only to ascribe importance to what the later serial works seemed to present, and treat the rest as "outworn". But the pretended "outworn" on one side and the prophetic aspects on the other constitute an ordered whole, the purpose of which will only be revealed if one dedicates oneself, without ideological ulterior motives, to a structural examination of his works. After this devoted work on Webern one will certainly have a better idea of the difference between him and the musicians who followed him.'[3] Ruwet alludes to the fact that Webern has been made the father of 'serial' music, music in which not only the actual notes but also other elements such as duration, dynamics, tone-colour, method of playing, octave pitch of individual notes and recently even intensity of

[1] *Reihe*, 2/38.   [2] p. 8.   [3] *Reihe*, 6/69.

vibrato have been organized serially; and this coupled with the assertion that Webern himself in his later works has arranged more things than the actual notes serially. This presents a further section of the Webern legend, a section which has already found its home in musical journalism. The beginning of this viewpoint could have been a lecture given in 1957 in Darmstadt by Luigi Nono, 'The Development of Serial Technique'.[1] He said: 'Schoenberg's idea of "serial composition" has been developed very much further in our time, in that now each individual element of music has been taken into consideration and subjected to the serial laws. So in the course of historical development twelve-note writing, which at first was limited to thematic elements, has gradually encroached upon the whole territory of musical composition and all its factors: pitch, rhythm, dynamics, tone-colour and form, and finally also on the element of time, as a function of which all the factors named above are present. Between the beginnings of twelve-note music and its present position there is an absolute historical and logical continuity of development. . . . In a letter which Anton Webern wrote to Willi Reich on 3 May 1941 explaining his Variations Op. 30[2] one can see the new musical ideas which are characteristic of the second stage of development of serial technique. . . . The constructive function of the series no longer deploys itself in relation to the characteristic thematic shape of the series. The construction of the Variations Op. 30 closely follows the twelve-note series in rhythm, timbre, melodic elements and harmonic elements. . . . The third stage of serial composition is in full development: the serial principle regulates every element of the composition in such a way that exact exchange between the different elements is possible. The twelve notes of the chromatic scale are arranged in series which either produce permutations in themselves or are derived from permutations or fixed combinations of the other elements. Sound is studied and analysed for the first time according to its natural construction, so that it can be immediately used in the composition of electronic music. This new phase of study, evolving logically from the earlier one, demands a new, more

[1] *Darmstädter Beiträge*, 1958/25.   [2] Quoted on p. 155.

progressive understanding of music—that of our future.' Nono
says on p. 34: 'We will now look at the musical works—especially
of recent years—of those composers who can perhaps be called
the "Darmstadt School". . . .' With this he has established the
place in the history of music, not only of his fellow-fighters in
the *avant-garde*, but also of himself. Nono, who in this attempt
to construct a logical development from Schoenberg through
Webern to Boulez, Stockhausen and Nono is clearly building on
Stockhausen's wrong analysis of Webern's Op. 24,[1] adds a new
mistake of his own by finding a serial organization of rhythm
too in Op. 30. In 1959 Zillig took over this point of view:[2]
'While Schoenberg, after his enormous step into atonality found
the new organization of the twelve-note system, and from this
organization achieved a classicism which had its exact correspondence in Beethoven, even if the musical material was entirely
different, in his use of the twelve-note system Webern did not go
back to the synthesis of atonality with the achievements of the
classic masters. He went on further. He was the first person to
make an intuitive application of the serial system, which Schoenberg only used for harmonic and melodic phenomena, to rhythm,
to the successive entries of voices, even to the dynamics, the tone-
colour and even the expression of each individual note. He freed
himself from thematic elements in the classical sense and replaced
it by something which the young composers today call Structure.' And he continues on p. 191: 'Webern now tried to control
all the factors which previously had been left to the free will of
the composer by the law of the series: i.e. the duration of the
individual notes, the dynamics, in which a rest is equated with
the dynamic value of nought and so acquires an entirely new
relationship to the sounded notes, and even the tone-colour of
the notes, which is conditioned in the orchestra by the division
between instruments and on the piano by the method of
performance.'

It is continually being demonstrated that this viewpoint is
wrong, as is being clearly shown by more exact analyses. Two
examples: 'The appeal to specially refined methods of composition

[1] *Permutation.*   [2] *Variationen*, p. 180.

in Webern and his exaltation as the real "Father of serialism" is so widespread among the musical *avant-garde* of our time that after listening to or reading such assertions one is inclined to assume that their authors have the most fundamental knowledge of Webern's spiritual personality and his complete works. But closer acquaintance with their compositions clearly shows that their calling on Webern is mostly derived from analyses of a few works undertaken from a prejudiced point of view and from the adoption of some slogans which do not originate from him.'[1] 'It would be a mistake to think that Anton Webern was already aiming at such "ordering in time". What Webern brought into being was a functional system of note- and motif-connections which worked within their own fundamental terms of reference. . . . Four years after Webern's death Olivier Messiaen wrote a work for piano—*Mode de Valeurs et d'Intensités*—which was based on a complete serial model, the first ever to apply to more than one dimension. Messiaen therefore did not arrive at the work's organization unconsciously, and then derive from it an abstract system: his insight consisted of applying an a priori method to give form to musical data in the three parameters pitch, duration and loudness, aiming at the best and most musical solution.'[2]

Boulez also agrees with Eimert about Webern's position, but ascribes the broadening of the treatment of the series to himself and other composers of the younger generation: 'My music has been strongly influenced by Webern, Debussy and Stravinsky. These are my ancestors, but I consider that music cannot have a different evolution from that given to it by Webern. With the Viennese composers the serial technique applies only to the pitch of the notes. My companions and I have extended it to all the components of the sound, the duration, timbre and method of attack. This is what I call total organization of sound, for all the components of the sound are thus organized.'[3] In the USA Milton Babbitt seems to have tried something of the kind before Messiaen, which is indeed very probable, as total mathematical determina-

[1] Willi Reich, *Schweizerische Musikzeitung*, 1960/320.
[2] H. Eimert, *Reihe*, 3/3.　　[3] *The World of Music*, 1952/12.

tion of music goes back with reasonable certainty to Schillinger, whose ideas only became known in Europe somewhat later.

With Pousseur both views of Webern's position in the development of music can be found: here one notices the misleading use in German of the French term 'serial', which Metzger has recently discussed:[1] 'Attempts have been made to discuss Webern's poetry in terms of a particular handling of twelve-note series. This made it necessary to regard the pre-serial period as one of preparation for the serial works and the latter [here Pousseur means the "normal" serial works] as a first attempt towards a generalized serialism such as Webern never in fact imagined':[2] and further: 'Webern not only sensed the possibilities of generalizing the serial system, he undertook to apply them.'[3] And Eimert has given a different version of his viewpoint, though very carefully formulated: 'Webern was the first composer to move on from the single-level conception of the twelve-note technique: namely that of a technique of organizing pitch levels. In his work, for the first time, we see the beginnings of a three-dimensional row technique—of what, in short, we know as serial technique. Webern restricted his music to the interval and the single note, and composed structures which are not in the traditional sense developed in a continuum, but which proceed by autonomous "leaps", leaps which in the pre-electronic stage could achieve everything but that final step from the bounds of instrumentally tempered sound. Only in electronic music has the real sense of these developments been realized.'[4] Since these lines were written, Webern, because of his allegedly 'serial' works, has been considered the father of electronic composition. It is as arbitrary as understandable that electronic music regarded a serially determined totality as the only thing adequate for it: confronted with the enormous possibilities of producing electronic sounds and their hitherto unknown possibilities of metrical differentiation, only a great creative personality could hold his own. Thus the flight into mathematics—or rather into compositional procedures which could be manipulated by mathematics—appears as the only

[1] Reihe, 5/25. [2] Reihe, 1955, 2/51.
[3] Reihe, 1957, 3/47. [4] Reihe, 1955, 1/8.

way out for lesser spirits from the over-plenty of uncontrolled material. But Anton Webern has nothing to do with all this.

When the young composers discovered Webern for themselves in the early 1950s it was inevitable that the few gifted characters who took up the stimulating influence of Webern's work productively and developed it further were surrounded by a large number of less inspired musicians who also swam in the fashionable pointillist stream and managed to keep above water for some time. Their chances were the greater because the bare scores of some of the master's late works appeared relatively easy to look through. Analytical examination of Webern was reduced in many cases to a method which Stadlen[1] compared with the linguistic method of counting the 'ands' and 'buts' in the Bible. The results of these were then exposed graphically in technical diagrams, the simplification of which seemed to make the successful imitation of Webern's style a possibility even for less gifted people. The results did not take long to appear in the music of festival programmes. The clear-sighted Boulez recognized the danger early on: 'The misunderstanding which awaits us and which we must very much distrust is that of confusing composition with organization.'[1] Craft in his introduction to the recording speaks of 'the mechanical so-called Webernites' and Stuckenschmidt said: 'The danger of an academicization of the radicalism of twelve-by-the-dozen style is the chief problem of young composers today: clearly it is only possible to escape it by exploding the rigid rule-book.'[3] But this radicalism produced by mechanically learnt methods is no longer daring. 'Avant-gardism has become a special profession. As its courage is well honoured it lacks any tragic characteristics.'[4] Especially because, as the permanent revolution is a powerful stimulus for the snob, avant-gardism is consciously cultivated. 'If many important positions of influence are in the hands of people who are always favourably disposed towards innovation for any reason and therefore, perhaps often against their conscious will, demand sensationalism, as is often the case in Europe today, then each of them is in danger of being con-

[1] *Score*, 25/66.   [2] Gavoty/Lesur, *Pour ou contre*, p. 71.
[3] *Melos*, 1958/204.   [4] Doflein, *Prisma*, p. 56.

tinually overtaken.'[1] Herzfeld has remarked on the unfortunate fact that a certain kind of criticism which has been attacked by a sort of Hanslick-complex hardly dares to state its own opinion any more and prefers to praise a dozen mediocrities rather than misjudge a potential genius.[2]

In this situation, where certain Webernians have gradually become a great danger as regards the proper results of Webern's work, the successful practitioners of the imitation of Schoenberg, Berg and Webern have been sharply criticized: 'These use the stylistic elements derived from expressionism and long robbed of their potential content as harmless work-tools deprived of their individual value. It is like children playing on the grass, where once there were houses and streets, with mine cases and splinters, ten years after the bomb attack, and laying them in rows and counting them and swapping them and giving them a fictitious value. . . . These composers in fact are mostly worthy fellows in the best of health, who travel in sleeping-cars, give lectures, tell jokes and take part in well-intentioned congresses: the desperation which produced the greatness of a *Pierrot Lunaire* or a *Wozzeck* has nothing to do with them.'[3] And Hans Werner Henze, without naming Webern, has dedicated a 'satire' to his imitators, a little masterpiece in speech of 'deep meaning'. This says:

> It can easily happen that someone is impaled on the points of the citizens' umbrellas, a victim of the stubborn fear of truth. Ten years later a first-class funeral is arranged, when everyone has busied themselves with truth. That is also the moment when the dead great man begins to form a school and start an academicism. Countless zealous scribes proclaim his mission, which he himself never had the chance to proclaim. Many students fall under his spell and reproduce in themselves the emotions of the former great man. What for him was the bold leap, the telegraph message from a high, distant station, the sounding again of the tender cry of the bird of death seen only by him—all this is now turned into brittle pointillist

[1] Křenek, *Komponist im Exil.*   [2] *Musica nova,* p. 256.
[3] Fedele d'Amico, *Melos,* 1956/133.

studies. The blood quickly dries up. Favourable moment: the people have not yet understood and there are still not many who agree with him: but very many people who do not wish to be regarded as belonging to the past are already on the side of the composer who had not yet had his true deserts. In the shadows of the evening the industrious students rush noisily on to the Piazza, in order to proclaim the ideas of the dead man in banal caricature and petty silliness as the doctrine of tomorrow. The doctrine of tomorrow is the death of the idea. The solitary man, who did not have more time to speak to his murderers, becomes an example of failure among men who walk uselessly up and down in front of closed windows. The creative sorrow of the One man is changed into general brooding on number relationships. Creative resistance is weakened in face of the material and finally gives up altogether. Even this capitulation takes place in the name of the One. The followers, pleased with their finds, turn his innocent, questioning expressions into woodenly lifeless abstractions. They are insensitive: possessing the sterile security of the academics, they arm themselves against all attacks from above and below. They are in the middle. A small encapsuled bourgeoisie inside the bourgeoisie. Lack of imagination keeps away any need for lack of safety. Contact with the uncertain is cut off.[1]

Stockhausen has already linked his profession of faith in Webern to the need to return from the imitation of his external stylistic elements. 'At the moment when one approaches the roots of Webern's music, one also reaches the stage of insight into its uniqueness and completeness and its vulnerability to any attempt at reproduction.'[2] But Webern

> ... becomes a yardstick: no composer can be active with a clear conscience, now or in the future, below the level of this music's language. ... Everyone ought to be aware of the solicitude and artistry with which Webern went to work on his material: how he left nothing out of account and achieved a stylistic purity which is the precondition for great art of any

[1] *Gefahren in der neuen Musik.*   [2] *Reihe*, 2/38.

time. . . . If in the most recent developments the ostensibly 'advanced' opinion has been put forward that Webern too is now 'passé'—as a few years ago we were told 'Schoenberg is dead'—this can only trouble those for whom Webern is a principle of composition and not an artist whose imperishable achievement redeemed his time and eased its transition to the ensuing one.

This refers to developments which are still in full spate. Where they will lead we do not know. But we know the direction. In a letter of 6 August 1928 to Hildegard Jone, Webern said: 'So I am entirely in agreement with you, when you say: We must come to believe that it only goes on further within us.'

WEBERN BIBLIOGRAPHY

ADORNO, THEODOR WIESENGRUND
Berg and Webern—Schoenberg's heirs (*Modern Music*, 1931, No. 8)
Anton Webern (Lecture on Südwestfunk, 21 April 1932; also *Schweizer. Musikzeitung*, 1932/679, and *Auftakt*, 1936/159)
Philosophie der Neuen Musik (Tübingen, 1949)
Postscript to the Insel Edition of Schoenberg's Op. 15
Zur Vorgeschichte der Reihenkomposition (in *Klangfiguren*, Berlin, 1959)
Anton von Webern (in *Klangfiguren*, Berlin, 1959)
Das Altern der Neuen Musik (in *Dissonanzen*, Göttingen, 1956)

ASUAR, JOSÉ VINCENTE
Una incursion por el op. 5 de Anton Webern (*Revista Musical Chilena*, 1958/19)

BABBITT, MILTON
Some aspects of twelve-tone-composition (*Score*, 12/53)

BAK, KEES
Over de 'Miskenning' von Anton Webern (*Mens en Melodie*, 1958/299)

BALDENIUS, IMKE
Stiluntersuchungen an den Opera 3, 4, 16, 17, 18 und 29 Anton Weberns (Thesis for the Künstl. Lehramt, Hamburg, 1959)

BAMBERGER, ECKENARD
Die Zwölftonalität; Versuch einer Kritik (Diss., Univ. of Innsbruck, 1957)

BARRAQUÉ, JEAN
Essays über Weberns Klaviervariationen (*Melos*, 1961/187)

BARUCH, GERTH-WOLFGANG
Anton von Webern (*Melos*, 1953/337)

BEALE, JAMES
Weberns musikalischer Nachlass (*Melos*, 1964/297)

BECKMANN, DORIS
Sprache und Musik bei Anton Webern (Diss., Univ. of Cologne, 1963)

BERENDT, J. A., and UHDE, J. (ed.)
Prisma der gegenwärtigen Musik (Hamburg, 1959)

BORRIS, SIEGFRIED
Über Wesen und Werden der neuen Musik in Deutschland (Berlin, 1948)
Stilistische Synopsis—Analogien und Kontraste (in *Stilporträts der Neuen Musik*, Berlin, 1961)
Strukturanalyse von Weberns Symphonie op. 21 (Congress report, Cassel, 1962/253)
Anton von Webern, Persönlichkeit und Werk (*Musik im Unterricht*, Ausg. B, 1966/293)

BOUCOURECHLIEV, ANDRÉ
La musique électronique (*Esprit*, 1960/98)

BOULEZ, PIERRE
Alea (*Darmstädter Beiträge*, 1958/44)
Eventuellement . . . (*Revue Musicale*, 1952, 212/117)
Hommage à Webern (*Domaine musical*, 1954/123)
Moment de J.-S. Bach (*Contrepoints*, VII/72)
Trajectoires: Ravel, Stravinsky, Schoenberg (*Contrepoints*, VI/122)
Tendances de la musique récente (*Revue Musicale*, 1957, 236/28)
(All these articles reprinted in *Relevés d'Apprenti*, Paris, 1966.)

BOUR, ERNEST
Die richtige Antwort (*Melos*, 1959/169)

BRADSHAW, MERRILL K.
Tonal Structure in the Early Works of Anton Webern (Diss., Univ. of Illinois, 1962)

BRAUNER, RUDOLPH FRANZ
Österreichs Neue Musik (Vienna, 1948)
Vom Dreiklang zum Zwölftonakkord (Vienna, 1949)

BRESGEN, CESAR
In memoriam Anton v. Webern in Mittersill (Ms)
Anton Webern in Mittersill (*Öst. Mus. Zs.*, 1961/226)
In memoriam Anton Webern (*Musikerziehung*, 1965/66)

BRINER, ANDRES, see under WEBERN

BROEKEMA, ANDREW J.

A Stylistic Analysis and Comparison of the Solo Vocal Works of Arnold Schoenberg, Alban Berg and Anton Webern (Ann Arbor, M.F. 62–4822)

CAPPELLI, IDA

Webern rückt in die erste Reihe auf (*Melos*, 1962/377)

Webern e l'Espressionismo (*Musica Università*, Rome, September 1964)

CASTIGLIONI, NICCOLÒ

Sul rapporto tra parola e musica nella II Cantata di Webern (*Incontri Musicali*, No. 3, Milan, 1959)

Entstehung und Krise des tonalen Systems (*Melos*, 1960/369)

CAVALLINI, EDOARDO

Dodecafonia e pluricromatismo (*Rivista Musicale Italiana*, 1950, Vol. 3)

CERHA, FRIEDRICH

Die Wiener Schule und die Gegenwart (*Öst. Mus. Zs.*, 1961/302)

CLARKE, HENRY LELAND

The Abuse of the Semitone in Twelve-tone Music (*Musical Quarterly*, 1959/295)

COLLAER, PAUL

Musique moderne (Brussels, 1955)

CRAFT ROBERT

Anton Webern (Introduction to the recording Columbia K4L-232, and *Score*, 13/9)

Boulez and Stockhausen (*Score*, 24/54)

DAHLHAUS, CARL, and STEPHAN, RUDOLF

Eine 'dritte Epoche' der Musik? Kritische Bemerkungen zur elektronische Musik (*Deutsche Univ. Zeitung*, 1955, Vol. 17)

DALLAPICCOLA, LUIGI

Incontro con Anton Webern (*Il Mondo*, Florence, 3 November 1945); also, as 'Begegnung mit Anton Webern' (*Melos* 1965/115)

DALLIN, LEON

Techniques of Twentieth Century Composition (Dubuque, 1957)

D'AMICO, FEDELE
Spiele mit Bombensplittern (*Melos*, 1956/130)
DANGEL, ARTHUR
Studien zu den 'Fünf Sätzen für Streichquartett' op. 5 von
Anton von Webern (Ms. 1958)
DIMOV, BOSCHIDAR
Webern und die Tradition (*Öst. Mus. Zs.* 1965/411)
DÖHL, FRIEDHELM
Studien zur Kompositionstechnik und -ästhetik Anton
Weberns (Examination paper, Freiburg i.br., 1961)
Weberns op. 27 (*Melos*, 1963/400)
Die Welt der Dichtung in Weberns Musik (*Melos*, 1964/88)
DORIAN, FREDERICK DEUTSCH
Webern als Lehrer (*Melos*, 1960/101)
DUMESNIL, RENÉ
La Musique Contemporaine en France (Paris, 1949)
EHRENFORTH, KARL HEINRICH
Schönberg und Webern. Das XIV. Lied aus Schönbergs
Georgelieder op. 15 (*Neue Zs. f. Musik*, 1965/102)
EIMERT, HERBERT
Lehrbuch der Zwölftontechnik (Wiesbaden, 1950)
Der Komponist und die elektronischen Klangmittel (*Musik-
leben*, 1954/242)
A Change of Focus (*Reihe*, 2/29)
Interval Proportions. String Quartet, 1st movement (*Reihe*,
2/93)
Die zweite Entwicklungsphase der Neuen Musik (*Melos*, 1960/
365)
The Composer's Freedom of Choice (*Reihe*, 3/1)
Die Reihe. Information über serielle Musik. Vol. 2, Anton Webern
(Vienna, 1955), in collaboration with Karlheinz Stockhausen
Critical discussions of above:
PETER STADLEN, Webern Symposium (*Score*, 25/66)
HELMUT SCHMIDT-GARRÉ (*Melos*, 1956/216)
RUDOLF STEPHAN (*Musikforschung*, 1956/364), Attack by
Eimert (*Musikforschung*, 1956/510), Defence by Stephan
(*Musikforschung*, 1957/334)

EMERY, ERIC
La gamme et le langage musical (Paris, 1961)
ERPF, HERMANN
Vom Wesen der Neuen Musik (Stuttgart, 1949)
Wie soll es weitergehen? (Rodenkirchen, 1958)
EVANS, EDWIN
Anton Webern (in *Cobbett's Cyclopedic Survey of Chamber Music*, London, 1930)
FANO, MICHEL
Situation de la musique contemporaine (*Domaine musical*, 1954/58)
FAURE, MAURICE
Une nouvelle écoute (*Esprit*, 1960/22)
FORNEBERG, ERICH
Der Geist der Neuen Musik. Der neue Klang im Spiegel der traditionellen Harmonielehre (Würzburg, 1957)
FORTNER, WOLFGANG
Anton Webern und unsere Zeit (*Neue Züricher Zeitung*, 1958; also *Melos*, 1960/325, and Lindlar, W. Fortner, Rodenkirchen, 1960)
FÜSSL, KARL HEINZ
Selbstbesinnung am Beispiel Strawinskys (*Öst. Mus. Zs.*, 1958/465)
GAVOTY, BERNARD, and LESUR, DANIEL
Pour ou contre la musique moderne (Paris, 1957)
GERHARD, ROBERTO
Tonality in Twelve-Tone Music (*Score*, 6)
Developments in Twelve-Tone Technique (*Score*, 17/61)
Twelve-Tone Technique in Strawinsky (*Score*, 20/38)
Apropos Mr Stadlen (*Score*, 23/50)
Die Reihentechnik des Diatonikers (in *Musik der Zeit*, Vol. 1, Bonn, 1958)
See also under WEBERN
GOEBEL, WALTER F.
Weberns Sinfonie (*Melos*, 1961/359)
GOLÉA, ANTOINE
Esthétique de la musique contemporaine (Paris, 1954)

Rencontres avec Pierre Boulez (Paris, 1958)
Rencontres avec Olivier Messiaen (Paris, 1960)

GREDINGER, PAUL
Serial Technique (*Reihe*, 1/38)

GRUBE, GUSTAV
Konzertkritik (*Musikalisches Wochenblatt/Neue Zs. f. Musik*, 1907/963)

GURVIN, OLAV
Fra tonalitet til atonalitet (Oslo, 1938)
Some Comments on Tonality in Contemporary Music (*Årbok for Norsk Musikgranskning*, 1954/55)
Ny musik in Norden (Stockholm, 1954)

HAMILTON, IAIN
Alban Berg and Anton Webern (in *European Music in the Twentieth Century*, London, 1957)

HEISS, HERMANN
Elemente der musikalischen Komposition (Heidelberg, 1949)
Musikalische Kombinatorik (*das neue forum*, 1959/60, p. 268)

HENZE, HANS WERNER
Gefahren in der neuen Musik (*Zs. Texte und Zeichen*, 1955, I/2); also in *Die Stimme der Komponisten* (Rodenkirchen, 1958)

HERZFELD, FRIEDRICH
Musica nova (Berlin, 1954)
Der Reiz des Krebses (*Neue Zs. f. Musik*, 1955/71)
Anton Weberns Tod (*Neue Zs. f. Musik*, 1958/147)

HEUSS, ALFRED
Vom Stand der heutigen Komposition in Deutschland (*Neue Zs. f. Musik*, 1928/383)

HODEIR, ANDRÉ
La musique étrangère contemporaine (Paris, 1954)
La Musique occidentale post-webernienne (*Esprit*, 1960/65)

ISENSEE, WOLF
A. Schönbergs op. 16, A. Bergs op. 6 und A. Weberns op. 6. Ein Vergleich (Thesis for the Künstl. Lehramt, Hamburg, 1959)

JACOBS, PAUL

L'interprétation (*Domaine musical*, 1954/67)

JELINEK, HANNS

Anleitung zur Zwölftonkomposition (Vienna, I/1952; II/1958)

JOACHIM, HEINZ

Revolution in Permanenz? Darmstädter Ferienkurse für Neue Musik (*Melos*, 1954/258)

KANDINSKY, WASSILY

Über das Geistige in der Kunst (Berne,[4] 1952)

KARKOSCHKA, ERHARD

Zur Entwicklung der Kompositionstechnik im Frühwerk Anton Weberns (Diss., Univ. of Tübingen, 1959)

KELLER, HANS

The Audibility of Serial Technique (*Monthly Musical Record*, November, 1955)

KELLER, WILHELM

Handbuch der Tonsatzlehre (Regensburg, I/1957; II/1959)

KETTING, OTTO

Anton Webern, persona non grata in Nederland (*Mens en Melodie*, August, 1958)

KIRCHMEYER, HELMUT

Strawinsky. Zeitgeschichte im Persönlichkeitsbild (Regensburg, 1958)

KLAMMER, ARMIN

Webern's Variations for Piano, Op. 27, 3rd movement (*Reihe*, 2/81)

KOLMAN, PETER

Anton Webern, der Schöpfer der Neuen Musik (*Slovenska hudba*, Vol. VII, No. 10)

KOLNEDER, WALTER

Klangtechnik und Motivbildung bei Webern (Annales Universitatis Saraviensis, Philosophie-Lettres IX-1-1960, p. 27, Müller-Blattau-Festschrift)

Stilporträt Anton Webern (in *Stilporträts der Neuen Musik*, Berlin, 1961)

Weberns Passacaglia op. 1. Zum Problem retrospektiver Analyse (Ms)

KŘENEK, ERNST

Freiheit und Verantwortung ('*23*' *Eine Wiener Musikzs.*, February 1934; also in *Zur Sprache gebracht*)

Über neue Musik. Sechs Vorlesungen zur Einführung in die theoretischen Grundlagen (Vienna, 1937)

Selbstdarstellung (Zürich, 1948)

De rebus prius factis (in *Die Stimme der Komponisten*, Rodenkirchen, 1958)

Der ganze Webern in drei Stunden (*Melos*, 1957/304)

Bericht über Versuche in total determinierter Musik (*Darmstädter Beiträge*, 1958/17)

LEEUW, TON DE

Symmetrie bei Webern (*Sonorum Speculum*, 20/14)

LEIBOWITZ, RENÉ

Le silence d'Anton Webern (*Labyrinthe*, Geneva, 15 November 1945)

Anton Webern (*L'Arche*, 1945, Vol. 11)

Schoenberg and his School (New York, 1949)

The Tragic Art of Anton Webern (*Horizon*, 1947/282)

Aspects récents de la technique de douze sons (*Polyphonie*, 1948, Vol. 4, p. 32)

Qu'est-ce que la musique de douze sons. Le concerto pour neuf instruments op. 24 d'Anton Webern (Liège, 1948)

Les Oeuvres Posthumes d'Anton Webern (in *Significations des Musiciens Contemporains*, Liège, 1949)

Introduction à la musique de douze sons (Paris, 1949)

LE ROUX, MAURICE

L'introduction à la musique contemporaine (Paris, 1947)

LESUR, DANIEL

See under GAVOTY

LEWINSKI, WOLF-EBERHARD VON

Young Composers (*Reihe*, 4/1)

LIESS, ANDREAS

Die Musik im Weltbild der Gegenwart (Lindau, 1949)

Die Stimme des Orients (*Musica*, 1960/769)

LIGETI, GYÖRGY

Metamorphoses of Musical Form (*Reihe*, 7/5)

Über die Harmonik in Weberns erster Kantate (*Darmstädter Beiträge*, 1960/49)

Weberns Melodik (*Melos*, 1966/116)

Die Komposition mit Reihen und ihre Konsequenzen bei Anton Webern (*Öst. Mus. Zs.*, 1961/297)

LINDLAR, HEINRICH

Musik der Einsamkeit. Zum 75. Geburtstag Anton von Weberns (*Deutsche Zeitung*, Cologne, 29 November 1958)

LINKE, KARL

Anton von Webern und Alban Berg (in Programmheft *Das musikfestliche Wien*, Vienna, 1912; also in WILLI REICH, *Alban Berg*, Zürich, 1959; London, 1964)

LIPPMANN, EDWARD ARTHUR

Webern: The Complete Music. Recorded . . . (*The Musical Quarterly*, 1958/416)

MARIE, JEAN ETIENNE

Musique vivante (Paris, 1953)

MCKENZIE, W. C.

The Music of Anton Webern (Diss., Univ. of Denton, Texas, 1960)

MELICHAR, ALOIS

Musik in der Zwangsjacke. Die deutsche Musik zwischen Orff und Schönberg (Vienna, 1958)

Schönberg und die Folgen. Eine notwendige kulturpolitische Auseinandersetzung (Vienna, 1960)

MERSMANN, HANS

Moderne Musik (Potsdam, 1927)

Neue Musik in den Strömungen unserer Zeit (Bayreuth, 1949)

METZGER, HEINZ-KLAUS

Webern and Schönberg (*Reihe*, 2/42)

Analysis of the Sacred Song Op. 15 No. 4 (*Reihe*, 2/75)

Intermezzo I (*Reihe*, 4/63)

Abortive Concepts in the Theory and Criticism of Music (*Reihe*, 5/21)

Hommage à Edgard Varèse (*Darmstädter Beiträge*, 1959/54)

MOLDENHAUER, HANS
The Death of Anton Webern (New York, 1961, Phil. Libr.)
Das Webern-Archiv in Amerika (*Öst. Mus. Zs.*, 1965/422)
Anton von Webern: Perspectives (Univ. of Washington, 1966)

NESTLER, GERHARD
Die Form in der Musik (Freiburg, 1954)
Der Stil in der Neuen Musik (Freiburg, 1958)

NONO, LUIGI
Die Entstehung der Reihentechnik (*Darmstädter Beiträge*, 1958/25)
Geschichte und Gegenwart in der Musik von heute (*Darmstädter Beiträge*, 1960/41)

OGDON, WILBUR LEE
Series and structure. An investigation into the purpose of the twelve-note row in selected works of Schoenberg, Webern, Křenek and Leibowitz (Diss., Univ. of Bloomington, Indiana, 1955)

PANNAIN, GUIDO
Origine e significativo della Musica dodecafonica (*Nuovo Antologia*, September 1954, p. 79)

PAULI, HANSJÖRG
Zur seriellen Struktur von Igor Strawinskys *Threni* (*Schweizer, Musikzeitung*, 1958/450)

PAZ, JUAN CARLOS
Arnold Schoenberg o, El fin de la era tonal (Buenos Aires, 1958)

PERLE, GEORGE
Serial Composition and Atonality (London, 1962)
Theory and Practice in Twelve-tone Music (*Score*, 25/58)
Atonality and the Twelve-note System in the United States (*Score*, 27/51)

PESTALOZZA, LUIGI
Storicità di Anton Webern (*La Rassegna Musicale*, 1958/303)

PFROGNER, HERMANN
Die Zwölfordnung der Töne (Zürich, 1953)

PHILIPPOT, MICHEL
Liberté sous conditions (*Domaine musical*, No. 1/24)
Anton Webern (*Cahiers Musicaux*, No. 5)

POCIEJ, BOHDAN
Gedankenmusik (*Ruch muzyczny*, 1965, Vol. 24; and 1966, Vol. 4)

POHLMANN, PETER
Die harmonischen Ordnungsprinzipien der neuen Musik, dargestellt an ihren Hauptvertretern (Diss., Univ. of Hamburg, 1956)

POUSSEUR, HENRI
Formal Elements in a New Compositional Material (*Reihe*, 1/30)
Anton Webern's Organic Chromaticism. 1st Bagatelle Op. 9 (*Reihe*, 2/51)
Outline of a Method (*Reihe*, 3/44)
Da Schoenberg a Webern, una mutazione (*Incontri musicali*, No. 1)
Webern und die Theorie (*Darmstädter Beiträge*, 1958/38)
Theorie und Praxis in der neuesten Musik (*Darmstädter Beiträge*, 1959/15)
Forme et pratiques musicales (*Revue Belge de Musicologie*, 1959/98); also, as 'Musik, Form und Praxis. Zur Aufhebung einiger Widersprüche' (*Reihe*, 6/71)
Vers un nouvel univers sonore (*Esprit*, 1960/52)

PRIEBERG, FRED K.
Es gibt keine 'neue' Musik (*Melos*, 1954/310)
Lexikon der Neuen Musik (Freiburg, 1958)

PRINGSHEIM, KLAUS
Zwischen Helmholtz und Schönberg (*Schweizer Musikzeitung*, 1959/385)

PUTZ, WERNER
Studien zum Streichquartettschaffen von Hindemith, Bartok, Schönberg und Webern (Diss., Univ. of Cologne, 1966; *Kölner Beiträge zur Musikforschung*, Vol. 36)

REDLICH, HANS FERDINAND
Alban Berg (London, 1957)

REICH, WILLI
Anton von Webern (*De Muziek*, 1929/30, p. 249)

Alban Berg und Anton von Webern in ihren neuesten Werken
(*Der Auftakt*, 1930/132)

Anton von Webern (*Die Musik*, 1930/812)

Anton von Webern (*Der Auftakt*, 1933/164)

Weberns Musik (in Special number of '23' *Webern zum 50.
Geburtstag*, February 1935; also contributions by Adorno,
Křenek, Jone and Humplik, Zenk and Rederer)

Alban Berg (Vienna, 1937)

Der 'Blauer Reiter' und die Musik (*Schweizer Musikzeitung*,
1945/341)

Per la morte di Anton Webern (*Il Mondo*, Florence, 2 February 1946)

Versuch einer Geschichte der Zwölftonmusik (in *Alte und neue
Musik*, Zürich, 1952)

Aus unbekannten Briefen von Alban Berg an Anton Webern
(*Schweizer Musikzeitung*, 1953/49)

Aus Alban Bergs Jugendzeit (*Melos*, 1955/33)

Alban Berg (Zürich, 1963; London, 1965)

Das Gesamtwerk Anton Weberns auf Schallplatten (*Schweizer
Musikzeitung*, 1960/320)

Anton Webern. Selbstzeugnisse und Worte der Freunde (Zürich,
1961)

Briefe aus Weberns letzten Jahren (*Öst. Mus. Ztg.*, 1965/
407)

Berg und Webern schreiben an Hermann Scherchen (*Melos*,
1966/225)

REICHENAU, KLAUS-PETER

Die Entwicklung des Kompositionsstils bei Anton Webern
(Examination paper, Univ. of Cologne, 1959)

RINGGER, ROLF URS

Wort-Ton-Bezeihung bei Anton Webern (*Schweizer Musikzeitung*, 1963, November/December Vol.)

Anton Weberns Klavierlieder (Diss., Univ. of Zürich,
1964)

ROCHBERG, G.

The Hexachord and Its Relation to the Twelve-Tone Row
(Pennsylvania, 1955)

ROCHE, MAURICE
Emploi fonctionnel du silence (*Esprit*, 1960/43)

ROGNONI, LUIGI
Espressionismo e dodecafonia (Milan, 1954)

RONDI, BRUNELLO
Il cammino della musica d'oggi e l'esperienza elettronica (Padua, 1959)

RUBIN, MARCEL
Webern und die Folgen (*Das Ton-Magazin*, 1961/41)

RUFER, JOSEF
Composition with Twelve Notes (London, 1954)
The Works of Arnold Schönberg (London, 1962)

RUWET, NICOLAS
Contradictions du langage sériel (*Revue Belge de Musicologie*, 1959/83); also, as 'Von den Widersprüchen der seriellen Sprache' ('Contradictions within the serial language') (*Reihe*, 6/59)

SCHAEFFER, PIERRE
A la recherche d'une musique concrète (Paris, 1952)

SCHÄFFER, BOGUSLAW
Nowa Muzyka (Cracow, 1958)
Präexistente und inexistente Strukturen (Congress report, Cassel, 1962/263)

SCHERCHEN, HERMANN
Dépassement de l'orchestre (*Revue musicale*, 1956/57, No. 236/56)

SCHILLINGER, JOSEPH
The Schillinger System of Musical Composition (New York, 1941)
The Mathematical Basis of Arts (New York, 1948)

SCHLOEZER, B. DE, and SCRIABINE, M.
Problèmes de la musique moderne (Paris, 1959)

SCHMIDT-GARRÉ, HELMUT
Zwölftonmusik—Ende einer Entwicklung, nicht Neubeginn (*Melos*, 1952/10)
Webern als Angry Young Man. Aus alten Zeitungskritiken über Anton Webern (*Neue Zs. f. Musik*, 1964/132)

See also under EIMERT

SCHNEBEL, DIETER
Die Variationen für Klavier von Anton von Webern. Eine
Anleitung zum Hören des Werkes (Ms. 1950)
Anton Webern (Ms. 1955)

SCHNIPPERING, HEINRICH
Von der Logik der Zwölftonmusik (*Melos*, 1950/312)

SCHOENBERG, ARNOLD
Harmonielehre (Leipzig, 1911)
Letters, selected and edited by Erwin Stein (London, 1964)

SCRIABINE, M.
See under SCHLOEZER

SCHWARZ, RUDOLF
Webern und Berg (*Musikblätter des Anbruch*, October 1924)

SEARLE, HUMPHREY
Webern's Last Works (*The Monthly Musical Record*, 1946/231)
Twentieth Century Counterpoint (London, 1954)
Webern (in FRIEDRICH WILDGANS, *Anton Webern*, London,
1966)

SIEVERS, GERD
Anton von Webern zum Gedenken (*Musica*, 1954/20)

SIOHAN, ROBERT
Horizons sonores. Evolution actuelle de l'art musical (Paris,
1956)

SLONIMSKY, NICOLAS
Music since 1900 (New York,[3] 1949)

SOURIS, ANDRÉ
Notes sur le rythme concret (*Polyphonie*, 1948/5)

SPINNER, LEOPOLD
Analysis of a Period (*Reihe* 2/46)
*A Short Introduction to the Technique of Twelve-tone Compo-
sition* (London, 1960)
Aus Weberns Kantate Nr. 2, Opus 31. Die Formprinzipien der
kanonischen. Darstellung (Analyse des vierten Satzes)
(*Schweizer Musikzeitung*, 1961/303)

STADLEN, PETER
Serialism reconsidered (*Score*, 22/12)

See also under EIMERT, WEBERN

STEFAN, PAUL

Neue Musik und Wien (Vienna, 1921)
Arnold Schönberg (Vienna, 1924)

STEIN, ERWIN

Alban Berg and Anton von Webern (*The Chesterian*, 1922/33)
Neue Formprinzipien (*Schönbergheft des Anbruch*, 1924)
Anton Webern, Fünf Stücke für Orchester (*Pult und Takt-stock*, 1926/109)
Weberns Trio op. 20 (*Neue Musikzeitung*, 1928/517)
The art of Anton Webern (*The Christian Science Monitor*, Boston, 22 June 1929)
Anton Webern (Obituary) (in *Orpheus in New Guises*, London, 1953)

STEPHAN, RUDOLF

Über einige geistliche Kompositionen Anton von Weberns (*Musik und Kirche*, 1954/152)
Anton von Webern (*Deutsche Univ. Zeitung*, 1956, Vol. 13/14)
Neue Musik (Göttingen, 1958)
See also under DAHLHAUS, EIMERT

STOCKHAUSEN, KARLHEINZ

Das Konzert für 9 Instrumente op. 24 (*Melos*, 1953/343)
For the 15th September 1955 (*Reihe*, 2/37)
Structure and Experiential Time (*Reihe*, 2/64)
Musik in Funktion (*Melos*, 1957/249)

STRAVINSKY, IGOR

Neue Dialogue: Igor Strawinsky—Robert Craft (*Melos*, 1958/261)

STROBEL, HEINRICH

So sehe ich Webern (*Melos*, 1965/285)

STUCKENSCHMIDT, HANS HEINZ

Neue Musik (Berlin, 1931)
Arnold Schönberg (London, 1960)
The 3rd Stage (*Reihe*, 1/11)
Musik gegen jedermann (*Melos*, 1955/245)
Verfall des musikalischen Geschmacks (*Öst. Mus. Zs.*, 1955/277)

Anton von Webern (in *Schöpfer der Neuen Musik*, Frankfurt/ Main, 1958)

Anton von Weberns Bild, zurechtgerückt zum 75. Geburtstag (*Frankfurter Allg. Zeitung*, 3 December 1958)

Deutung der Gegenwart (*Archiv für Musikwissenschaft*, 1959/ 246)

TIPPETT, MICHAEL
Moving into Aquarius (London, 1959)

UHDE, J.
See under BERENDT

VELTEN, KLAUS
Anton Weberns Lied op. 4 Nr. 5

VENUS, DANKMAR
Vergleichende Untersuchungen zur melodischen Struktur der Singstimmen in der Liedern von A. Schönberg, A. Berg, A. Webern und P. Hindemith (Diss., Univ. of Göttingen, 1965)

VLAD, ROMAN
Modernità e tradizione nella musica contemporanea (Milan, 1955)

Anton von Webern e la composizione atematica (*La Rassegna Musicale*, 1955/98)

Storia della dodecafonia (Milan, 1958)

VOORTHUYSEN, J. VAN
Anton Webern's complete œuvre (*Symphonia*, 1959/81)

WANGERMÉE, ROBERT
La Musique belge contemporaine (Brussels, 1959)

WEBERN, ANTON
Heinrich Isaac: Choralis Constantinus Part 2, edited by A. von Webern (*DTO*, XVI/1, Vienna, 1909)

Schönbergs Musik (in *Arnold Schönberg*, Munich, 1912)

Letters of Webern and Schoenberg to Roberto Gerhard (*Score*, 24/36)

Briefe an Hildegard Jone und Josef Humplik, ed. Josef Polnauer (Vienna, 1959)

The Path to the New Music, ed. W. Reich, containing *The Path to the New Music*, 8 lectures, 1933

The Path to Twelve-Note Composition, 8 lectures, 1932
Postscript with letters to W. Reich (Vienna 1960)
Critical discussions of above:
ROBERTO GERHARD, Some lectures by Webern (*Score*, 28/25)
ANDRES BRINER, An den Wurzeln eines neuen musikalischen Stils (*Schweizer Musikzeitung*, 1961/15)
PETER STADLEN, Die Webern-Legende (*Musica*, 1961/66)

WESTERGAARD, PETER
Webern and Total Organisation (*Perspectives of New Music*, New York, 1963)

WESTPHAL, KURT
Die moderne Musik (Berlin, 1928)
Das Publikum und die Neue Musik (in *Musikstadt Berlin zwischen Krieg und Frieden*, Berlin, 1956)

WILDBERGER, JACQUES
Webern gestern und heute (Programme, Donaueschingen, 1959)

WILDGANS, FRIEDRICH
10 Jahre Ferienkurse für Neue Musik in Darmstadt (*Öst. Mus. Zs.*, 1955/263)
Anton von Webern. Zu seinem 75. Geburtstag am 3. Dezember 1958 (*Öst. Mus. Zs.*, 1958/457)
Gustav Mahler und Anton von Webern (*Öst. Mus., Zs.*, 1960/302)
Anton Webern, a Biography (London, 1966)

WOLFF, CHRISTIAN
Movement (*Reihe*, 2/61)

WOLFF, PIERRE
La Musique Contemporaine (Paris, 1954)

WOLPERT, F. A.
Neue Harmonik (Regensburg, 1951)

WÖRNER, KARL H.
Neue Musik in der Entscheidung (Mainz,[2] 1956)
Neue Musik 1948–1958. Versuch eines historischen Überblicks (*Darmstädter Beiträge*, 1959/7)

ZILLIG, WINFRIED
Anton Webern, Aussenseiter und Vorbild (in *Variationen über neue Musik*, Munich, 1959)
Zur Geschichte der Neuen Musik. Von der Dodekaphonie zur Elektronik (*Musica*, 1960/777)

Addendum
BRINDLE, REGINALD SMITH
Serial Composition (London, 1866)

WEBERN'S WORKS

WITH OPUS NUMBERS

All of the works with opus numbers (except 13a and 14a) are
published by Universal Edition A.G., Karlsplatz 6, Vienna 1,
Austria.

Opus

1 *Passacaglia for Orchestra* (1908)
2 *Entflieht auf leichten Kähnen* (Stefan George), for mixed
   chorus a cappella (1908)
3 *Five Songs* (from *Der siebente Ring* by Stefan George), for
   medium voice and piano (1907–8)
4 *Five Songs* (Stefan George), for high voice and piano
   (1908–9)
5 *Five Movements for String Quartet* (1909). Also arranged for
   string orchestra (1929)
6 *Six Pieces for Large Orchestra*: First version (1910); Second
   version (1928)
7 *Four Pieces for Violin and Piano* (1910)
8 *Two Songs* (Rainer Maria Rilke), for medium voice, clarinet
   (bass clarinet), horn, trumpet, celesta, harp, violin, viola,
   and cello (1910)
9 *Six Bagatelles for String Quartet* (1913)
10 *Five Pieces for Orchestra* (1911–13)
11 *Three Small Pieces for Cello and Piano* (1914)
12 *Four Songs*, for high voice and piano (1915–17)
13 *Four Songs for Soprano and Orchestra* (1914–18)
13a The same, version for voice and piano
14 *Six Songs* (George Trakl), for high voice and instruments
   (1917–21)
14a The same, version for voice and piano
15 *Five Sacred Songs*, for soprano and instruments (1917–22)
16 *Five Canons on Latin Texts*, for high soprano, clarinet, and
   bass clarinet (1923–24)

17 *Three Sacred Folksongs* (Three Traditional Rhymes) for voice, violin (viola), clarinet, and bass clarinet (1924)

18 *Three Songs*, for voice, E flat clarinet, and guitar (1925)

19 *Two Choral Songs* (Goethe), with instruments (1926), Mixed chorus (SATB), clarinet, bass clarinet, celesta, guitar, violin

20 *String Trio* (1927), Violin, viola, cello

21 *Symphony* (1928)

22 *Quartet*, (1930), clarinet, tenor saxophone, violin, piano

23 *Three Songs* from *Viae inviae* by Hildegard Jone, for medium voice and piano (1934)

24 *Concerto for Nine Instruments* (1934), flute, oboe, clarinet, horn, trumpet, trombone, violin, viola, piano

25 *Three Songs* (Hildegard Jone), for high voice and piano (1934–35)

26 *Das Augenlicht* (Hildegard Jone), for mixed chorus and orchestra (1935)

27 *Variations for Piano* (1936)

28 *String Quartet* (1938)

29 *First Cantata* (Hildegard Jone), for soprano solo, mixed chorus, and orchestra (1938–39)

30 *Variations for Orchestra* (1940)

31 *Second Cantata* (Hildegard Jone), for soprano and bass soli, mixed chorus, and orchestra (1941–43)

WITHOUT OPUS NUMBERS

The nine items published are shown as follows:

CF: Carl Fischer, Inc., 62, Cooper Square, New York 10003 (Boosey and Hawkes, Regent St., London)

UE: Universal Edition A.G., Karlsplatz 6, Vienna I, Austria

BB: Boelke-Bomart Music Publications, Inc., Hillsdale, New York

Opera

Alladine und Palomides, Maeterlinck (1908), sketch

Orchestra

Im Sommerwind, idyll for large orchestra (1904) [CF]

Four Pieces (ca. 1910–13)
'Kräftig bewegt', F major
'Sehr bewegt', D major
Composition for string orchestra, D minor
Two movements in A minor
Voice and Orchestra
   Siegfrieds Schwert, ballade for solo voice and orchestra (1903)
   'O sanftes Glühn der Berge' (1913)
   Two Songs (1914)
   'O Mutter, Dank! So fühl ich deine Hand' (1919), sketch
Wind and String Instruments
   Composition (1925)
String Quartet
   Langsamer Satz (1905) [CF]
   Quartet (1905) [CF]
   Quartet in A minor, sketches
   Rondo
   Minuet and Trio in A minor
   'Sehr bewegt'
String Trio
   Satz für Streichtrio (1925) [UE]
   String Trio (1925), sketch
Quintet
   Quintet for string quartet and piano (1906) [BB]
Violin and Piano
   Extensive piece
Violoncello and Piano
   Two Pieces (1899)
   Sonata (1914)
Piano Solo
   Satz für Klavier (ca. 1905–6), sketches
   Kinderstück (1924)
   Sonatensatz (ca. 1906)
   Varia
Songs, Voice and Piano
   Three Poems (1899–1903) [CF]
   Vorfrühling II (Avenarius), draft

Two Songs after Poems by Ferdinand Avenarius (1900–1)
Three Songs after Poems by Ferdinand Avenarius (1903–4)
[CF]
Eight Early Songs (1901–4) [CF]
'Liebeslied' (Hans Böhm) (1904), fragment
Five Songs after Poems by Richard Dehmel (1906–8) [CF]
Four Songs after Poems by Stefan George (1908–9)
Early songs (uncatalogued)
Hochsommernacht, duo (Martin Greif)
Chorales
German chorales

ARRANGEMENTS

Three items are published to date by Universal Edition.

J. S. BACH
Ricercare a 6 voci (1935) (UE), No. 2 in *The Musical Offering*

FRANZ SCHUBERT
Deutsche Tänze (UE)
'Romanze' from *Rosamunde*, voice and orchestra
'Ihr Bild', voice and orchestra
'Der Wegweiser', voice and orchestra
'Du bist die Ruh', voice and orchestra
'Thränenregen', voice and orchestra
Three sonata movements, orchestra

HUGO WOLF
'Der Knabe und das Immelein', voice and orchestra
'Denk es, o Seele!', voice and orchestra
'Lebe wohl', voice and orchestra

ARNOLD SCHOENBERG
Sechs Orchesterlieder, Opus 8 (No. 1), (Nos. 2 and 6)
Kammersymphonie, Opus 9 (UE)
Friede auf Erden, Opus 13
Fünf Orchesterstücke, Opus 16
Gurrelieder: 'Vorspiel'

Three Folksongs
Four German Folksongs

Unidentified
'Zum Schluss', voice and orchestra

INDEX

Adler, Guido, 15, 20–1, 177
Adorno, T. W., 30fn., 32, 54, 60, 83, 104fn., 110–11, 119, 149fn., 158, 172, 180, 181fn., 186, 189, 194

Babbitt, Milton, 200
Bach, David Josef, 97, 186
Bach, J. S., 25, 28, 95, 123, 143, 152, 155, 164, 167–75
Bad Ischl, 16
Balanchine, George, 78
Baldenius, Imke, 105
Barcelona, 123, 186
Barlach, Ernst, 91
Bartók, Béla, 19, 34, 36, 42, 58, 73, 74, 126, 144fn.
Baruch, Gerth-Wolfgang, 24, 25
Basle, 50, 80, 122, 136fn., 151
Bauch, Hinner, 167
Bayreuth, 16, 20
Beethoven, 21, 27, 29, 55, 96, 120, 130, 140, 155, 184, 199
Berg, Alban, 18, 21, 23, 24, 32, 45, 62, 71, 80, 81fn., 112, 120fn., 158, 164, 178–81 passim, 183, 203
  correspondence, 16, 30, 82, 120, 192
  relationship with Webern, 15, 69, 124, 165, 186, 189
  works, 53, 58–60 passim, 62, 183, 203
Berlin, 16, 61, 176, 187fn.
Bethge, Hans, 81
Blaue Reiter, 34, 54
Blavatsky, Helena, 190
Bochum, 17
Borris, Siegfried, 114fn., 117, 142
Boulez, Pierre, 172–3, 182fn., 195–6, 199, 200, 202
Boyden, David, 12
Brahms, 21, 22–3, 25, 27, 29, 123, 130, 140, 143, 163, 182, 184
Bresgen, Cesar, 188, 191–3 *passim*
Brücke, 34
Bruckner, 55
Busoni, 140fn.

Canon, 31, 89–91, 92–6, 115–17, 159, 177
Casella, Alfredo, 144fn.
Castiglioni, Niccolò, 98
Clark, Edward, 186
Complementary harmony, 31–2, 47, 71–2, 79, 125
Coolidge, Elizabeth Sprague, 144
Cowell, Henry, 36
Craft, Robert, 12, 24, 25fn., 26, 67–8, 173, 202

Dahlhaus, Carl, 134
Dallin, Leon, 121–2
D'Amico, Fedele, 203fn.
Danzig, 16
Darmstadt (Kranichstein Summer School), 134, 171, 194, 196, 198, 199
David, J. N., 9
Debussy, 58, 64, 126, 176, 200
Dehmel, Richard, 34
Diez, Ernst, 20
Doflein, 202fn.
Dorian, F. D., 21fn., 183–6
Dornach, 136fn.
Dowling, Lyle, 133–4

Eckermann, 140
Eimert, Herbert, 26, 104, 105–6, 146–7, 151, 153–4, 180, 187fn., 188, 200, 201
Eisler, Hanns, 179
Electronic music, 73, 134, 201
Erpf, Hermann, 12

Fauves, 34
Frederick the Great, 167
Freud, 182
Fürstenfeld, 30

Gavoty, Bernard, 202fn.
George, Stefan, 30, 33, 34, 36, 49, 50, 52, 54, 59, 66, 105
Gerhard, Roberto, 183
Gesualdo, Carlo, 27
Goethe, 20, 81, 97, 117, 136, 140, 160, 191

229

INDEX

INDEX

INDEX